The George
and Helen
Ladd Library

■

BATES COLLEGE

LEWISTON, MAINE

The Writer's FAQs

A POCKET HANDBOOK

MURIEL HARRIS
Purdue University

Prentice Hall
Upper Saddle River
New Jersey 07458

Library of Congress Cataloging-in-Publication Data

Harris, Muriel
    The writer's FAQs : a pocket handbook / Muriel Harris.
      p.   cm.
    Includes index.
    ISBN 0-13-021025-0
    1. English language—Rhetoric—Handbooks, manuals, etc.
  2. English language—Grammar—Handbooks, manuals, etc.
  3. Report writing—Handbooks, manuals, etc.   I. Title.
  PE1408.H3458 2000
  808'.042—dc21   98-50348
                                                      CIP

Editorial Director: Charlyce Jones Owen
Editor in Chief: Leah Jewell
Director of Production and Manufacturing: Barbara Kittle
Senior Production Manager: Bonnie Biller
Production Editor: Joan E. Foley
Copyeditor: Anne F. Lesser
Editorial Assistant: Patricia Castiglione

Manufacturing Manager: Nick Sklitsis
Prepress and Manufacturing Buyer: Mary Ann Gloriande
Director of Marketing: Gina Sluss
Marketing Manager: Brandy Dawson
Associate Creative Director and Cover Designer: Carole Anson
Interior Design: Circa 86

To Sam, David, Bekki, Dan, and Hannah . . .
As Always and Ever

Grateful acknowledgment is made to the following reviewers:
  Kenneth E. Claus, Florida International University;
  Margaret J. Marshall, University of Pittsburgh;
  Geri Rhodes, Albuquerque Technical-Vocational Institute;
  and Kenneth C. Thompson, George Mason University.

This book was set in 8/11 Serifa by Carlisle Communications Inc. and was printed and bound by R.R. Donnelley & Sons Company.

© 2000 by Prentice-Hall Inc.
Upper Saddle River, New Jersey 07458

Printed in the United States of America
10 9 8 7 6 5 4 3 2 1

ISBN 0-13-021025-0   (paper)
ISBN 0-13-021399-3   (spiral wire)

Prentice-Hall International (UK) Limited, *London*
Prentice-Hall of Australia Pty. Limited, *Sydney*
Prentice-Hall Canada Inc., *Toronto*
Prentice-Hall Hispanoamerica, S.A., *Mexico*
Prentice-Hall of India Private Limited, *New Delhi*
Prentice-Hall of Japan, Inc., *Tokyo*
Pearson Education Asia Pte. Ltd., *Singapore*
Editora Prentice-Hall do Brasil, Ltda., *Rio de Janeiro*

How to Use This Book

Keep this book nearby to help you find answers to your writing questions in the quickest, easiest manner possible.

■ Before you start
Read the "Writing" part for reminders, advice, and writing tips.

■ As you write a draft of your paper
For sentence structure:
Check "Sentence Choices" for suggestions for general sentence construction, clarity, word choice, and smooth flow.

For research papers and finding information:
The "Research" section offers advice on choosing a topic, finding information, using the library, evaluating and integrating sources into your paper, and avoiding plagiarism.

For going online:
The "Online" section will help you use search engines efficiently, locate useful resources, evaluate and cite them, and find Web addresses to lead you to useful starting places.

■ As you write a bibliography or reference list
For your list of sources, you'll find explanations for MLA, APA, *Chicago Manual of Style,* and Council of Biology Editors (CBE) in "Documentation." See "Online" for online citations.

■ As an ESL student looking for information on using English
If you are a multilingual speaker (ESL=English as a Second Language), the whole book is useful as a guide for all writers. But questions that don't come up for native speakers are in the "Multilingual Speakers (ESL)" part and in ESL HINT boxes.

■ As you finish up and are editing and polishing a draft
When you are ready to check a point of grammar and mechanics, use "Sentence Grammar," "Punctuation," and "Mechanics" for the frequently used rules of grammar, spelling, capitalization, and other matters that indicate to readers that you're a literate user of the English language and that your ideas have merit. But what do you do if, like many writers, you can tell when something *isn't* right, but aren't sure what *is* right? Read on because this book is designed to help.

How do you find what you're looking for?

■ If you know the term (or want to check on a term)
1. Go to the Index at the back of the book.
2. Go to the Glossary of Usage and Glossary of Terms near the end of the book.

■ If you know the general topic (such as using commas)
1. Find the topic in the Brief Contents inside the front cover.

2. Read the descriptions listed here and then do the following:
   a. Browse in the Brief Contents.
   b. Look at the questions at the beginning of that part.
   c. Turn to the list of questions inside the back cover.

Writing Suggestions on writing concerns, linking sentences and paragraphs, writing introductions and conclusions, and so on.

Sentence Choices Information on writing clear, effective sentences that don't overuse the passive, and are varied, concise, and nonsexist in word choices.

Sentence Grammar Grammar rules to help you avoid errors such as fragments, comma splices, and so on.

Punctuation Guidelines for punctuation marks as well as a useful diagram indicating the punctuation patterns for sentences.

Mechanics Guidelines for capitalization, use of italics, numbers, abbreviations, and spelling.

Multilingual Speakers Help with questions about English that ESL students are likely to have.

Research Papers Advice and guidelines for moving through the research paper process.

Online Help with going online to find, evaluate, and document information.

Documentation Guidelines for documentation formats.

Glossary of Usage Questions about word choices (Do I use "accept" or "except"?) and whether a certain word is acceptable in standard English (Can I write "and etc."?).

Glossary of Terms Definitions of grammatical terms (such as "linking verb" or "reflexive pronoun") and charts to illustrate terms such as "personal pronouns" and "sentence diagram."

■ **If you have a question**
1. If it's about one of those sticky word choices (for example: Is it "affect" or "effect"? Should I write "it's" or "its"?), go to the Glossary of Usage near the end of the book.
2. If the question is one that writers frequently have (the kind where you don't quite know the terminology to use), go to the inside back cover of the book and see if your question is like one of those FAQs (Frequently Asked Questions).

You'll also find HINT boxes throughout the book offering advice to avoid various problems writers encounter. Other user-friendly aids are lists and diagrams to help explain and clarify. As the term "user-friendly" implies, I hope this book is easy to use and becomes a writing friend that you keep nearby as you write.

Muriel Harris

Writing

The section in this part of the book offers help with general writing processes and answers the following questions:

1 Checklist for Effective Papers

HOCs (Higher Order Concerns)

Listed here are the Higher Order Concerns (HOCs) that help make your writing effective:

Purpose

Be sure your purpose fits the assignment. If you are asked to persuade your readers, that is different than writing to explain or summarize. If you are asked to describe, your purpose is to help your readers envision your subject. Read the assignment carefully, and note the verbs carefully. Are you asked to *compare* two or more things? *Analyze? State your opinion?*

You can clarify your purpose by answering the questions, "Why am I writing this? What am I trying to accomplish?" For example, do you want your readers to take some action? Accept your view? Understand something they didn't know before? Share some experience of yours?

Audience

Think about your readers. Check to see that they are the appropriate audience for your assignment and purpose. Think about what they already know and what they most likely want to know or don't need to know. Do you need to add any information or background summary to help them understand your topic?

If you are arguing or persuading, are you writing to those who are likely to disagree? If so, how can you convince them? Is there some common ground, some aspects of the argument you share with them, that will help in getting those who disagree to consider what you are writing?

Thesis statement

Your thesis is the main idea or subject of the paper. You should be able to summarize it briefly in a sentence or two, and your paper should state this clearly for the reader. Think of the thesis as a promise that you will discuss this topic—a contract you will fulfill. When you read over your draft, check to see you have kept all parts of your promise.

Organization

As you look over your draft, note the central idea of each paragraph (the topic sentence) and ask yourself if each paragraph contributes to the larger thesis in some way. Make an outline of the topic sentences and look over that organization to see if it is logical. You want to avoid gaps or jumps in the development of your thesis that might confuse the reader.

Development

Be sure you have enough details, examples, specifics, supporting evidence, and information to support your thesis. You may need to delete irrelevant material or add material that will strengthen your thesis and help you achieve your purpose.

Paragraph length

Paragraphs are the large building blocks of the paper. As you look over your draft, check to see that the paragraphs are of the same approximate length on the page. If you have a paragraph that takes most of a page, followed by a paragraph that has only a few sentences, you may need to make the paragraphs more equal in length.

Transitions between sentences and paragraphs

Transitions connect or knit sentences and paragraphs together into a smooth whole. Like road signals, they indicate where the writing is heading and keep your reader following along easily. Check to see that you've supplied the needed connectors to indicate how your writing is moving forward.

Introductions and conclusions

The introduction brings the reader into your world, builds interest in your subject, and announces the thesis or topic of the paper. Sometimes, writers write the introduction after revising the rest of the paper and clarifying their topic through their writing and revising.

The conclusion of the paper signals that the end is approaching and helps the reader to put the whole paper in perspective. You can either look backward and offer a conclusion that summarizes the content or look forward and offer advice, suggestions, or actions the reader can take, based on what you have presented.

LOCs (Later Order Concerns)

When you have finished your major revisions and checked the HOCs (page 2), look more closely at words, sentences,

LOCS (PROOFREADING CHECKLIST)

After your draft is well on the way to being completed, check for the Later Order Concerns (LOCs) as you edit and proofread.

and punctuation for problem areas that detract from your credibility as a writer. As you make your own list of problems to check for, consider whether you need to check for these common problems:

fragments	(see section 11, page 26)
subject-verb agreement	(see section 13, page 29)
verb endings	(see section 13, page 33)
verb tenses	(see section 13, page 37)
comma splices and fused sentences	
	(see section 12, page 28)
misplaced or omitted apostrophes	
	(see section 20, page 62)
pronoun reference	(see section 14, page 43)
omitted words	(see section 34, page 100)
omitted commas	(see section 19, page 59)
unnecessary commas	(see section 19, page 61)
spelling errors	(see section 28, page 85)

Strategies for checking on HOCs and LOCs

Find writing strategies that are effective for you, such as the following:

- Have someone (such as a tutor in your writing center) read your paper aloud as you listen and look at it, or read the paper aloud yourself. You'll see problems that are not as evident when you read silently.
- Put the draft away for a while so that when you read, the paper is not as fresh in your mind. To revise effectively, having some distance from the paper helps because you can more easily identify readers' concerns.
- Try to put yourself in the place of your intended readers and think about what they would want to know, what they might object to in your arguments, what counterarguments they would make, what questions they would have. Ask yourself if your paper responds adequately to these considerations.

■ For proofreading you need to help your eyes slow down and see each word. (Readers tend to see whole groups of words at once.) Try sliding a card down the page as you read because that permits your eyes and ears to work together.

■ Proofread for spelling by reading backward, either from the end of the paper to the beginning or from the right side of the line to the left. Then you are not focusing on the meaning of the sentences and can notice smaller matters such as word choice, punctuation, and spelling. Computer spell checkers catch some, but not all, spelling errors.

■ Don't depend on computerized grammar checkers. They may help slightly, but they cannot analyze language well enough to check completely for grammar problems, and the options suggested are sometimes not appropriate.

■ Draw up a personal list of problem areas and keep those in mind as you reread your draft.

Make a personal checklist here:

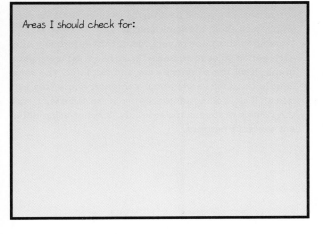

Areas I should check for:

Strategies for using computers

Word processing on a computer can help as you write and as you check your paper. Try the following strategies to see which are helpful for you:

■ Copy the topic sentences from each paragraph and put them in an outline onscreen. If you have any questions about the organization, cut and paste and see if other arrangements are more effective.

■ Be sure to use a spell checker because it is especially useful in catching typos. But remember that spell checkers can't find all spelling problems. They cannot, for example, distinguish between "it's" and "its" or "here" and "hear" to see if you have used the right form of these sound-alike words.

■ As you write, highlight in some way (such as boldface) problem areas or phrases that you have questions about. Then you can find them later and reconsider them.

■ If you think it might be better to delete a chunk of text, cut and paste it to a new file or to the end of the paper while you see if the paper is better without it. By putting it in a separate file, you can save it for later use or retrieve it if you decide you need it.

■ If a fresh idea pops into your mind as you're writing but probably belongs elsewhere in the paper, write that in a separate file. (Some word processing programs permit you to make notes to yourself as you write that are not visible in the main text.)

■ Many writers need to print out a hard copy of the paper as it develops to get a better sense of the whole paper.

■ To check on paragraph length, switch to page or print view so you can see a whole page on the monitor. See if the paragraphs look about the same length.

■ Working with a copy of your file, hit the return key after each period so each sentence looks like a separate paragraph. If all the sentences are approximately the same length, consider varying your sentences more (see section 4). If most of the sentences begin the same way (with the subject of the main clause), think about using different sentence patterns.

II

Sentence Choices

The sections in this part of the book discuss choices you make as you write. In most cases, there is no right or wrong answer, but you want to choose carefully so your writing is clear, concise, and smooth.

continued ▶

2 Clarity

Positive instead of negative

Put information in the positive because negative statements are harder to understand than positive ones.

Unclear negative: Less attention is paid to commercials that lack human interest stories.

Revised: People pay more attention to commercials with human interest stories.

Negatives can also make the writer seem evasive or unsure.

Evasive negative: Congresswoman Petros is not often heard to favor raising the minimum wage.

Revised: Congresswoman Petros prefers keeping the minimum wage at its present level.

Double negatives

Use only one negative at a time in your sentences. Double negatives are grammatically incorrect and may be difficult to understand.

Double negative: They don't want no phone calls.

Revised: They don't want any phone calls.

HINT

AVOIDING NEGATIVE WORDS

Watch out for negative words such as the following:

hardly	no place	nothing
neither	nobody	nowhere
no one	none	scarcely

They hardly had ~~no~~ ^{any} popcorn left.

Known information to new or unknown information

Start your sentences with information that is known or generally familiar to your reader before you introduce new or unknown material.

9

Familiar ⟶ Unfamiliar

Familiar to new: When I visit my grandmother, she often
                        has an old book from her childhood
                        days to show me.

(This sentence should be easy to understand.)

New to familiar: An old book from her childhood days is
                        something my grandmother often
                        shows me when I visit.

(This sentence takes longer to understand and is less clear.)

Verbs instead of nouns

Actions expressed as verbs are more easily understood and usually more concise than actions named as nouns.

Unnecessary noun forms: Pay raises are a motivation im-
                            provement.
Revised: Pay raises improve motivation.

Intended subject as sentence subject

The real subject or doer of the action in the verb should be the grammatical subject of the sentence. Sometimes the real subject can get buried in prepositional phrases or other less noticeable places.

HINT

USING VERBS INSTEAD OF NOUNS

Try rereading your sentences to see which nouns could be changed to verbs.

Some noun forms	Verbs to use instead
The determination of	They determine
The approval of	They approve
The preparation of	They prepare
The utilization of	They use
The analysis of	They analyze

Buried subject: It was the preference of the instructor to
                       begin each lecture with a quiz.

*(The grammatical subject here is it. Who begins each lec-
ture? The instructor.)*

Revised: The instructor preferred to begin each
                       lecture with a quiz.

3   Conciseness

To be concise, eliminate the following:

- what your readers do not need to know
- what your readers already know
- whatever doesn't further the purpose of your paper

Sometimes writers are wordy when they are tempted to include
everything they know about a subject, add a description of how
they found their information (to impress readers with how hard
they've worked to get the information), or add words they think
will make their writing sound more formal or academic.

  Strategies to eliminate unnecessary words:

- **Avoid repetition.** Some phrases, such as the following,
  say the same thing twice:

first beginning	9 A.M. in the morning
circular in shape	true facts
return again	really and truly
green in color	each and every

- **Avoid fillers.** Some phrases, such as the following, add little or nothing to your meaning:

in view of the fact that	due to the fact that
I am going to discuss	there are (or) is
the topic that I will explain here	

  T
  ~~I am going to discuss~~ *t*he cloning of human beings ~~, which~~
                                     ^
  is a subject that raises many difficult ethical questions.

- **Combine sentences.** When the same nouns appear in two
  sentences, combine the sentences.

and

Global warming is a critically important topic, ~~Global warming~~
has been the subject of recent TV specials, government
regulations, and conferences.

- **Eliminate** *who, which,* **and** *that.*

    The marking pen ~~that was~~ on my desk is gone.

- **Turn phrases and clauses into adjectives and adverbs.**

    The football player who was graceful = the graceful
    football player

    The building built out of cement = the cement building

    The entrance to the station = the station entrance

- **Remove excess nouns and change to verbs whenever possible.**

    agreed

    He ~~made the statement that he was in agreement with the concept~~ that inflation could be controlled.

- **Use active rather than passive.** (See section 7, page 15.)

    research department

    The ~~figures were~~ checked ~~by the research department~~.

4 Variety

A series of short sentences or sentences with the same subject-
verb word order can be monotonous and sound choppy. Try
these strategies for adding variety.

- **Combine short, choppy sentences.** Connect two sentences into one longer sentence with one subject and two verbs, or a comma and coordinating conjunction, or a semicolon, (see sections 12, 13, 18, and 19).

    , and they

    The school band performed at the local Apple Festival. ~~They~~
    were a great success.

    Tuck a phrase, clause, or sentence inside a related sentence.

The school band performed at the local Apple , who

Festival, ~~They~~ were a great success. ,

- **Rearrange sentence order.** Often, a series of sentences that sound choppy all have a subject-verb-object order. You can make one sentence depend on another or add or change phrases and clauses to break up the monotonous sound.

Choppy: The reporter asked each candidate the same question. He wanted to compare their campaign promises. They all evaded his questions. He wrote a story about their lack of answers.

Revised: Because the reporter wanted to compare the candidates' campaign promises, he asked each one the same question. Hearing them evade his questions, he wrote a story about their lack of answers.

5 Voice (Formal and Informal)

In writing, an appropriate voice is one that fits the level of formality of your paper and your subject. Just as you don't wear a suit or dress when you go on a picnic or jeans to a formal dinner, you should match your word choices to the type of paper you are writing.

Formal documents such as research papers, reports, and applications avoid slang but may include some technical language, or jargon, appropriate to the field and the intended readers. Such documents are normally written in the third person, using "he" and "they."

Informal documents such as e-mail and letters to friends, informal essays, and some memos may include more informal word choices (for example, "kids" instead of "children") and frequent contractions, and they are normally written in the first person, using "I."

Compare these recommendations:

Informal: Be sure to see *Titanic.* I saw it last week, and it's great!

Formal: The laminate is the recommended choice for this product because test results show that it holds up well under stress and heat.

Slang

Slang words may be shared by a small group or may be generally known. Some slang enters the general vocabulary, such as "cab" or "yuppie," and some eventually disappears or becomes outdated, such as "far out" or "BMOC" (Big Man on Campus). It is usually too informal for most written work.

Jargon

Jargon words are specialized terms used by those in the same field or profession to refer quickly to complex concepts. For someone who is knowledgeable about computers, the terms "gigabytes" and "bit maps" are useful technical terms when writing to someone else in that field. Such shorthand vocabulary should only be used when you are sure your readers will be familiar with the words.

The term "jargon" is also applied to pompous language that is inflated and unnecessarily formal. The result is wordy prose that is hard to read and makes the writer sound pretentious.

Pompous: She was inordinately predisposed to render her perspective on all matters of national and international import.

Revised: She frequently offered her opinion on world affairs.

 **6** **Mixed Constructions**

Mixed constructions are caused by mismatches when fitting parts of a sentence together. A writer can start off in one direction and then switch to another, causing grammar or logic problems in the sentence.

Mixed: For groups who want to reduce violence on television, students carrying knives to school are acting out what they see on the television screen.

Revised: Groups who want to reduce violence on television claim that students carrying knives to school are acting out what they see on the television screen.

Dangling modifiers

Some mixed constructions are caused by dangling modifiers—phrases or clauses that should modify the subject but don't.

Dangling: After <u>finishing</u> her degree, the <u>search</u> for a job
began.

(This sentence says that the <u>search</u>, the subject of the sentence, <u>finished</u> her degree.)

Revised: After <u>finishing</u> her degree, <u>she</u> began the
search for a job.

Mismatched subjects and predicates

Sometimes the subject and predicate don't match or fit together.

Mismatched: <u>Driver education</u> in high schools <u>assumes</u>
that parents can pay the costs involved.

(<u>Driver education</u>, the subject, can't make assumptions about anything.)

Revised: High school administrators assume that
parents can pay the costs involved for
driver education programs.

7 · Active and Passive Verbs

An active verb expresses the action completed by the subject. A passive verb expresses action done to the subject.

The active voice is usually more direct, clearer, and more concise than passive. However, sometimes the passive is a better choice.

Active: Paul drove the car.

(The verb is <u>drove</u>, and <u>Paul</u>, the subject, did the driving.)

Passive: The car was driven by Paul.

(The verb is <u>was driven</u>, and <u>the car</u>, the subject, was acted upon.)

Active verbs are clearer than passive because they indicate who is doing the action and add a better sense of immediateness and vigor. In a sentence with a passive verb, the "by the" phrase where the doer of the action is indicated may be left out or put far from the verb. Compare these sentences:

Passive: The photographs showing the tornado were
snapped in a hurry by me.

Active: I hurriedly snapped the photographs of the tornado.

Because active verbs add directness and force, they are often a better choice for sentences containing action that begin with "there is" or "there are."

Original	Revised
There were six victims of the crime whose accounts of what happened agreed.	Six of the crime victims gave the same accounts of the crime.

However, there are occasions to use the passive:

- When the doer of the action is not known or not important:

  The water temperature was recorded.

- When you want to focus on the receiver of the action:

  Historical fiction is not widely read.

- When you want to focus on the action, not the doer:

  The records have been destroyed.

- When you want to avoid blaming or giving credit:

  The candidate concedes that the election is lost.

- When you want a tone of objectivity or wish to exclude yourself:

  The complete report was drafted and on the president's desk yesterday.

8 Parallelism

Parallel structure exists when the same grammatical form or structure is used for equal ideas in a list or in a comparison. That similar form helps your reader locate the similar or compared ideas. Often, the equal elements repeat words or sounds.

Parallel: The computer manual explained how to boot
                                            (1)

up the hard drive and how to install the software.
                                            (2)

(Phrases (1) and (2) are parallel because both start with how to.)

Parallel: Watching Walt fumble with his headgear was
                                        (1)

as funny as seeing him try to skate.
                           (2)

(Phrases (1) and (2) are parallel because both start with -ing verb forms.)

Parallel: Three keys to marketing success include the
                 following:

1. To listen to the customer's wishes
         (1)
2. To offer several alternatives
      (2)
3. To motivate the customer to buy
          (3)

(Phrases (1), (2), and (3) are parallel items in a list because all begin with to + verb.)

Parallel is also needed when you link items using the following:

both . . . as   either . . . or
not only . . . but   neither . . . nor
coordinating conjunctions: *for, and, nor, but, or, yet, so*
comparisons using *than* or *as*

Parallel: Job opportunities are not only increasing in
                                              (1)

the health fields but expanding in many areas
                         (2)
of manufacturing as well.

(1) and (2) are parallel items using -ing verbs linked with but.)

Faulty parallelism is not only grammatically incorrect but can also lead to possible lack of clarity.

Dr. Willo explained that either starting the
                                (1)

                        avoiding
treatment or ~~to avoid~~ surgery was impossible.
                  (2) ^

PARALLEL STRUCTURE

As you proofread, do the following:

- Listen to the sound when you are linking equal ideas
  or comparing two or more elements. (Parallelism can
  add emphasis to your writing and public speaking by
  that repetition of sound.)
- Visualize similar elements in a list and check to see if
  they are in the same grammatical structure.

Tara wondered whether it was better <u>to tell</u> her mother

(1)

to fix

that she had wrecked the car or maybe ~~fixing~~ it herself.

(2) ^

9 Transitions

Transitions are words and phrases that build bridges to connect sentences, parts of sentences, and paragraphs together. These bridges show relationships and add smoothness (or "flow") to your writing.

There are several types of transitions you can use:

Repetition of a key term or phrase

Delegates at the conference could not agree on the degree of danger from <u>global warming</u>. But no one disputed the existence of <u>global warming</u>.

Synonyms

The <u>movie industry</u> is expanding to produce a variety of forms of entertainment, such as television films and music videos. But <u>Hollywood</u> will always have movies as its main focus.

Pronouns

<u>College tuition</u> has been increasing rapidly for several years. But <u>it</u> still does not finance needed improvements on many campuses.

■ Transition words and phrases

The investigators looking into the cause of the pollution pinpointed one farm. <u>Therefore</u>, the owner was forced to reduce his use of the fertilizers that were washing into the stream. <u>In the meantime</u>, the local chemical plant continued its dumping practices.

HINT

WORDS THAT START SENTENCES

Although some instructors prefer that you don't use or overuse the transitions "But" or "And" as sentence starters, it is not wrong to use them. Any word can start a sentence.

TRANSITIONS

Adding:	and, besides, in addition, also, too, furthermore, third
Comparing:	similarly, likewise, in the same way, at the same time
Contrasting:	but, yet, on the other hand, instead, whereas, although
Emphasizing:	indeed, in fact, above all, and also, obviously, clearly
Ending:	after all, finally, in sum
Giving examples:	for example, for instance, namely, specifically, that is
Showing cause and effect:	thus, therefore, consequently, as a result, accordingly, so
Showing place or direction:	over, above, next to, beneath, to the left, in the distance
Showing time:	meanwhile, later, afterward, now, finally, in the meantime
Summarizing:	in brief, on the whole, in conclusion, in other words

10 Nonsexist Language

Language that favors the male noun or pronoun or excludes females is sexist. To avoid such language, do the following:

■ **Use alternatives to man:**

Man	Alternative
man	person
mankind	people, human beings
man-made	machine-made, synthetic
to man	to operate

■ **Use alternatives for job titles:**

Man	Alternative
chairman	chair, chairperson
mailman	letter carrier, postal worker
policeman	police officer
fireman	firefighter

Strategies for avoiding masculine pronouns:

■ **Use the plural instead.**

Sexist: Give the customer his receipt immediately.
Revised: Give customers their receipts immediately.

■ **Reword and eliminate the male pronoun.**

Sexist: Give the customer his receipt.
Revised: Give the customer the receipt.

■ **Replace the male pronoun with one, you, he or she, and so on.**

Sexist: The student can select his preferred residence hall.
Revised: The student can select his or her preferred residence hall.

■ **Address the reader directly.**

Sexist: The applicant should mail two copies of his form by Monday.
Revised: Mail two copies of your form by Monday.

USING EVERYONE . . . HIS

For indefinite pronouns such as "everyone" and "anybody," the traditional practice is to use the masculine singular to refer back to that pronoun:

Traditional: Everyone brought his own pen and paper.

To avoid the male pronoun, which is seen by many people as sexist, you can use the strategies just listed.
  Others, however, such as the National Council of Teachers of English, accept the plural as a way to avoid sexist language:

  Everyone brought their own pen and paper.

III

Sentence Grammar

The sections in this part offer help with grammatical rules for most common problems. If you are not familiar with certain grammatical terms, such as "fragment," "comma splice," "subject-verb agreement," or "pronoun reference," and want to look up the rules for these, check the glossary of terms at the back of the book, use the index to find the term you are looking for, or use the question section here.

continued ▶

11 Fragments

A sentence fragment is an incomplete sentence. To recognize a fragment consider the basic requirements of a sentence:

■ A sentence is a group of words with at least one independent clause.

■ An independent clause has a subject and complete verb plus an object or a complement if needed.

■ An independent clause can stand alone as a thought, even though it may need other sentences before and after it to clarify the thoughts being expressed.

Independent clause: Jeremy's picture was in the newspaper.

Independent clause: He scored six three-point baskets during the game.

(We don't know who "he" is in this sentence, but a pronoun can be a subject, and we don't know which game is being referred to. But those bits of information, if needed, would be explained in accompanying sentences. The clause has a subject ["he"], a verb ["scored"], and an object ["baskets"].)

Not an independent clause: Because he scored six three-point baskets during the game.

(Say that clause out loud, and you will hear that it's not a complete sentence. The problem is that we don't know the result of the "because" clause.)

Not an independent clause: Luis who was one of my closest friends in third and fourth grade and is now moving with his family to another city.

(This is not a complete sentence because it has a subject, "Luis," but no main verb that tells us what Luis did. The verbs "was" and "is moving" belong to another subject [the pronoun "who"] and tell us what "who" did.)

Some fragments are unintended:

Unintended fragment: There were some complications with her phone bill. Such as two calls she did not make and a long distance charge for a local call.

(The second sentence is an unintended fragment because it has no subject and verb. It is a phrase that got disconnected from the independent clause that came before it.)

Unintended fragment: The doctor's recommendation that I get more sleep because I was becoming very stressed out while taking too many classes which I need for my major.

(The subject is "recommendation" but there is no main verb to complete that thought.)

Some fragments are intentional when they are used to add an effect such as emphasis or sudden change in tempo. However, intended fragments should only be used when the writing clearly indicates that the writer chose to include a fragment.

AVOIDING FRAGMENTS

HINT 1

To proofread for fragments caused by misplaced periods, read your paper backward, from the last sentence to the first. You will notice a fragment more easily when you hear it without the sentence to which it belongs. Most, but not all, fragments occur after the main clause.

HINT 2

Some fragments are caused by a marker word typically found at the beginning of a dependent clause that requires a second clause to finish the thought. Consider a marker word such as "if" and how it affects the clause:

If A happens ⟶ ?

When you hear that, you want to know what B is, that is, what the result is if A happens.

    Watch for other, similar marker words such as the following:

after	before	since
although	even though	unless
because	if	when

Intended fragment: Never had there been such a deci-
                           sive victory in the school's history of
                           participating in the tournament, and
                           no one stayed at home that night
                           when the team's bus pulled into
                           town. <u>No one.</u>

(The fragment, "No one," is used here to add emphasis.)

12 Comma Splices and Fused Sentences

A comma splice and a fused sentence (also called a run-on sentence) are punctuation problems in compound sentences. (A compound sentence is one that joins two or more independent clauses—clauses that could have been sentences by themselves.)

To avoid comma splices and fused sentences, note the three patterns for commas and semicolons in compound sentences:

1. Join two independent clauses with a comma and one of the seven joining words (coordinating conjunctions) listed:

   Independent clause**,** for independent clause.

                           and
                           nor
                           but
                           or
                           yet
                           so

   No one was home, but the door was open.

2. Join two independent clauses with a semicolon and no joining words:
   Independent clause**;** independent clause.

   No one was home; the door was open.

3. Join two independent clauses with a semicolon and any connecting word other than one of the seven joining words for commas listed in number 1: for, and, nor, but, or, yet, so.
   Independent clause**;** however, independent clause.

                           therefore,
                           consequently,
                           thus,

No one was home; however, the door was open.

If you don't use one of these three patterns for compound sentences, the sentence will have a comma splice:

Comma splice: No one was home, the door was open.

USING COMMAS IN COMPOUND SENTENCES

HINT 1

When punctuating compound sentences, think of the comma as only half of the needed connection to tie two independent clauses together. The other half is the connecting word. You need both the comma and the connecting word.

HINT 2

Don't put commas before every "and" or "but" in your sentences. "And" and "but" have other uses in sentences in addition to joining two independent clauses.

 Subjects and Verbs

Subject-verb agreement

Subjects and verbs should agree in number and person.

■ To agree in number, the verb used with a plural subject should have a plural ending, and a verb used with a singular subject should have a singular ending.

The customer	orders
(singular subject)	(singular verb)

The customers	order
(plural subject)	(plural verb)

■ To agree in person, the verb should be in the same person (first person = I/we, second person = you, or third person = he/they) as the subject.

I know   you know   she knows   they know

(For verb tense endings, see page 33.)

■ Some subjects are hard to find because they are buried among many other words. In that case, disregard the prepositional phrases, modifiers, and other surrounding words.

Almost every <u>one</u> of the applicants for the job who

came for interviews <u>is</u> highly qualified.
(verb)

HINT

SUBJECT-VERB AGREEMENT

HINT 1

The letter -*s* is used both for subject endings (plural) and for verb endings (singular). Because a plural subject can't have a singular verb, and a singular verb can't have a plural subject, the letter -*s* should not normally be the ending for both subject and verb.

chimes ring   the chime rings

HINT 2

When you check subject-verb endings, start by finding the verb. The main verb is the word that changes when you change the time of the sentence, from past to present or present to past. Then, ask yourself "who" or "what" is doing that action, and you will find the subject.

HINT 3

To find a subject buried among other words and phrases, start by eliminating phrases starting with prepositions; "who," "that," or "which" clauses; or words such as the following:

including	along with	together with
accompanied by	in addition to	as well as
except	with	no less than

Compound subjects

Subjects joined by "and" take a plural verb (X and Y = more than one).

The (stereo) and the (speaker) are sold as a unit.

Sometimes, words joined by "and" act together as a unit and are thought of as one thing. If so, use a singular verb.

(Peanut butter and jelly) is his favorite sandwich spread.

Either/Or subjects

When the subject words are joined by "either . . . or," "neither . . . nor," or "not only . . . but also," the verb agrees with the closest subject word.

Either (Maylene) or her (children) are going to bed early.

Indefinites as subjects

Indefinite words with singular meanings such as "each," "every," and "any" take a singular subject when (1) they are the subject word, or (2) they precede the subject word.

Each (book) on the shelves is marked with a bar code.

However, when indefinite words such as "none," "some," "most," or "all" are the subject, the number of the verb depends on the meaning of the subject.

(Some) of the movie is difficult to understand.

(Some) of those movies are difficult to understand.

Collective nouns and amounts as subjects

Nouns that refer to groups or a collection (such as "family," "committee," or "group") are collective nouns. When the collective noun refers to the group acting as a whole or single unit, the verb is singular.

Our (family) needs a new car.

Occasionally, a collective noun refers to members of a group acting individually, not as a unit. In that case, the verb is plural.

The (committee) are happy with each other's decisions.

Plural words as subjects

Some words that have an *-s* ending, such as "news" or "mathematics," are thought of as a single unit and take a singular verb.

Physics is . . .   Economics is . . .   Measles is . . .

Some words, such as those in the following examples, are treated as plural and take a plural verb, even though they refer to one thing. (In many cases, though, there are two parts to these things.)

Jeans are . . .   Pants are . . .   Scissors are . . .

Titles, company names, and terms as subjects

For titles of written works, names of companies, and words used as terms, use singular verbs.

All the King's Men is the book assigned for this week.
General Foods is hiring people for its new plant.
"Cheers" is a word he often uses when leaving.

Linking verbs

Linking verbs agree with the subject rather than the word that follows (the complement).

Those (poems) are my favorites.

The (poem) is their favorite.

There is/There are/It

When a sentence subject is "there is," "there are," or "it," the verb depends on the complement that follows it.

There is a surprise (ending) to that story.

There are surprise (endings) in many of her stories.

Who, Which, That, and *One of . . . Who/Which/That* as subjects

When "who," "which," and "that" are used as subjects, the verb agrees with the previous word they refer to (the antecedent).

They are the (students) who want to change the parking rules.

He is the (student) who wants to change the parking rules.

In the phrase "one of those who," it is necessary to decide whether the "who," "which," or "that" refers only to the one or to the whole group. Only then can you decide whether the verb is singular or plural.

Mr. Liu is one of the (salespersons) who know the product.

(In this case, Mr. Liu is part of a large group, those sales-persons who know the product.)

Mr. Liu is the only (one) of the salespersons who knows the product.

Verbs

Regular and irregular verb forms

Verbs that add *-ed* for the past tense and the past participle are regular verbs:

I talk   I talked   I have talked
(present)   (past)   (past participle)

The past participle is the form that has a helping verb such as "has" or "had."

VERB FORMS (REGULAR)			
	Present	**Past**	**Future**
Simple	I walk	I walked	I will walk
Progressive	I am walking	I was walking	I will be walking
Perfect	I have walked	I had walked	I will have walked
Perfect Progressive	I have been walking	I had been walking	I will have been walking

VERB FORMS (IRREGULAR)

Verb	Present		Past	
	Singular	Plural	Singular	Plural
to be	I am you are he, she, it is	we are you are they are	I was you were he, she, it was	we were you were they were
to have	I have you have he, she, it has	we have you have they have	I had you had he, she, it had	we had you had they had
to do	I do you do he, she, it does	we do you do they do	I did you did he, she, it did	we did you did they did

Some of the frequently used irregular verb forms include the following:

IRREGULAR VERBS

Base (present)	Past	Past participle
awake	awoke	awoken
be	was, were	been
beat	beat	beaten
become	became	become
begin	began	begun
bet	bet	bet
bite	bit	bitten (or) bit
bleed	bled	bled
blow	blew	blown
break	broke	broken
bring	brought	brought
build	built	built
burst	burst	burst
buy	bought	bought
catch	caught	caught

Base (present)	Past	Past participle
choose	chose	chosen
come	came	come
cost	cost	cost
cut	cut	cut
dig	dug	dug
do	did	done
draw	drew	drawn
drink	drank	drunk
drive	drove	driven
eat	ate	eaten
fall	fell	fallen
feed	fed	fed
feel	felt	felt
fight	fought	fought
find	found	found
fling	flung	flung
fly	flew	flown
forbid	forbade	forbidden
forget	forgot	forgotten
freeze	froze	frozen
get	got	gotten
give	gave	given
go	went	gone
grow	grew	grown
hang	hung	hung
have	had	had
hear	heard	heard
hit	hit	hit
hold	held	held
hurt	hurt	hurt
keep	kept	kept
know	knew	known
lay	laid	laid
lie	lay	lain
make	made	made
mean	meant	meant
meet	met	met
mistake	mistook	mistaken
pay	paid	paid
prove	proved	proved (or) proven
put	put	put
read	read	read
ride	rode	ridden

Base (present)	Past	Past participle
ring	rang	rung
rise	rose	risen
run	ran	run
say	said	said
see	saw	seen
sell	sold	sold
send	sent	sent
set	set	set
shake	shook	shaken
shine	shone	shone
shoot	shot	shot
shrink	shrank	shrunk
shut	shut	shut
sing	sang	sung
sit	sat	sit
sleep	slept	slept
slide	slid	slid
speak	spoke	spoken
spend	spent	spent
spin	spun	spun
split	split	split
spread	spread	spread
spring	sprang	sprung
stand	stood	stood
steal	stole	stolen
stick	stuck	stuck
stink	stank	stunk
strike	struck	struck
swear	swore	sworn
sweep	swept	swept
swim	swam	swum
swing	swung	swung
take	took	taken
teach	taught	taught
tear	tore	torn
tell	told	told
understand	understood	understood
wear	wore	worn
weep	wept	wept
win	won	won
wind	wound	wound
write	wrote	written

Lie/lay; sit/set; rise/raise

Three sets of verbs that cause problems are "lie/lay," "sit/set," and "rise/raise." Because they are related in meaning and sound, they are sometimes confused with each other. In each case, one of the set takes an object and the other doesn't, and each member of the set has a somewhat different meaning:

Lie (recline)	She lies in bed all day. (present)
	She lay in bed all last week. (past)
Lay (put)	He lays his dishes on the table. (present)
	He laid his dishes on the table. (past)
Sit (be seated)	Please sit here by the window. (present)
	He sat by the window in class. (past)
Set (put)	Please set the flowers on the table. (present)
	He set the flowers on the chair before he left. (past)
Rise (get up)	They all rise early in the morning. (present)
	They all rose early yesterday too. (past)
Raise (lift up)	Can you raise that weight above your head? (present)
	He raised the curtain for the play. (past)

Verb tense

The four verb tenses for past, present, and future are as follows:

■ Simple:
   I see   I saw

■ Progressive: "be" + *-ing* form of the verb
   I am seeing   I was seeing

■ Perfect: "have," "had," or "shall" + the *-ed* form of the verb
   I have walked   I had walked

■ Perfect progressive: "have" or "had" + "been" + *-ing* form of the verb
   I have been singing   I had been singing

(For a guide to using the tenses, see section 30.)

Verb voice

Verb voice tells whether the verb is in the active or passive voice. In the active voice, the subject performs the action of the verb. In the passive voice, the subject receives the action.

VERB ENDINGS

Avoid the verb ending problem that omits the final "d" or uses "of" instead of "have" in such forms as the following:

might have <u>like</u> to (should be: might have <u>liked</u> to)

could <u>of</u> (should be: could <u>have</u>)

suppose to (should be: <u>supposed</u> to)

The doer of the action in the passive voice may be omitted or may appear in a "by the . . ." phrase.

Active: The child sang the song.

Passive: The song was sung by the child.

Verb mood

The mood of a verb tells whether it expresses a fact or opinion (**indicative** mood); expresses a command, request, or advice (**imperative** mood); or expresses a doubt, wish, recommendation, or something contrary to fact (**subjunctive** mood).

Indicative: The new software <u>runs</u> well on this computer.
Imperative: <u>Watch</u> for falling rock.
Subjunctive: In the subjunctive, present tense verbs stay in the simple base form and do not indicate the number and person of the subject. Use the subjunctive mood in "that" clauses following verbs such as "ask," "insist," and "request."

In the past tense, the same form as simple past is used; however, for the verb "be," "were" is used for all persons and numbers.

It is important that he <u>join</u> the committee.

He insisted that she <u>be</u> one of the leaders of the group.

If I <u>were</u> you, I wouldn't ask that question.

14 Pronouns

Pronoun case

Pronouns, the words that substitute for nouns, change case according to their use in a sentence.

Subject: <u>He</u> bought some film. It is <u>he</u>.
Object: Cherise gave <u>him</u> the film.
Possessive: No one used <u>his</u> film.

PRONOUN CASE						
	Subject		**Object**		**Possessive**	
	sing.	pl.	sing.	pl.	sing.	pl.
1st person	I	we	me	us	my, mine	our, ours
2nd person	you	you	you	you	your, yours	your, yours
3rd person	he	they	him	them	his	their, theirs
	she	they	her	them	her, hers	their, theirs
	it	they	it	them	it, its	their, theirs

Pronoun case in compound constructions

To find the right case when your sentence has two pronouns or a noun and a pronoun, temporarily eliminate the noun or one of the pronouns as you read the sentence to yourself. You will hear the case that is needed.

Which is correct?   Nathan and him ordered a pizza.
(or)
Nathan and he ordered a pizza.

   Test: Would you say "Him ordered a pizza"? The correct pronoun here is "he."

Which is correct?   I gave those tickets to Mikki and she.
(or)
I gave those tickets to Mikki and her.

COMMON PROBLEMS WITH PRONOUNS

HINT 1

Remember that "between," "except," and "with" are prepositions, and they take pronouns in the object case:

between you and me   (*not* between you and I)

except Amit and her   (*not* except Amit and she)

HINT 2

Possessive case pronouns never take apostrophes:

his shoes (*not* his' shoes)

its eye (*not* it's eye)

HINT 3

Don't use "them" as a pointing pronoun in place of "those" or "these." Use "them" only as the object by itself.

those pages (*not* them pages)

HINT 4

Use possessive case before *-ing* verb forms.

They applauded his scoring a goal. (*not* him scoring)

HINT 5

Reflexive pronouns are those that end in "*-self*" or "*-selves*" and are used to intensify the nouns they refer back to:

I soaked myself in suntan oil.

Please help yourself.

Don't use the reflexive pronoun in other cases because it sounds as if it might be more correct. (It isn't.)

        I
Joseph and ~~myself~~ went to pick up the tickets.
         ^

         me
They included ~~myself~~ in the group.
        ^

Test: Would you say "I gave those tickets to she"? When in doubt, some writers mistakenly choose the subject case, thinking it sounds more formal. But the correct pronoun here is "her," the object case, because it is the object of the preposition "to."

Who/Whom

In informal speech, some writers do not distinguish between "who" and "whom." But for formal writing, the cases are as follows:

Subject	Object	Possessive
who	whom	whose
whoever	whomever	

Subject: Who is going to drive that van?
Object: To whom should I give this booklet?
Possessive: Everyone wondered whose coat that was.

HINT

USING "WHO" AND "WHOM"

If you aren't sure whether to use "who" or "whom," turn a question into a statement or rearrange the order of the phrase:

Question: (Who, Whom) are you looking for?

Statement: You are looking for whom.

Sentence: She is someone (who, whom) I have already met.

Rearranged order: I have already met whom.

Pronoun case after "than" or "as"

In comparisons using "than" or "as," choose the correct pronoun case by recalling the words that are omitted:

He is taller than (I, me). (The omitted words are "am tall.")
He is taller than I (am tall).

My sister likes her cat more than (I, me). (The omitted words are "she likes.")
My sister likes her cat more than (she likes) me.

"We" or "us" before nouns

When combining "we" or "us" with a noun, such as "we players," use the case that is appropriate for the noun. You can hear that by omitting the noun and seeing which sounds correct.

(We, Us) players chose to pay for our own equipment.

Test: Would you say "Us chose to pay for our own equipment"? The correct pronoun here is "We."

"WE" OR "US"?

Remember the famous opening words of the U.S. Declaration of Independence: "We the people. . . ."

Pronoun case with infinitives ("to" + verb)

When using pronouns after infinitives, verb forms with "to" + verb, use the object case. (You can also hear this by omitting a noun that may precede the pronoun.)

She offered to drive Orin and (I, me) to the meeting.

Test: Would you say, "She offered to drive I to the meeting? The correct pronoun here is "me."

Pronoun case before gerunds (-*ing* verb forms)

If a pronoun is used to modify a gerund, an -*ing* word, use the possessive case.

She was proud of (us, our) walking in the fund-raising marathon.

The correct form here is the possessive "our."

Pronoun antecedents

Pronouns substitute for nouns. In the sentence "Emilio washed his car," the pronoun "his" is a substitute for the noun Emilio (to avoid unnecessary repetition) and refers back to Emilio. The noun that a pronoun refers back to is its antecedent. For clarity, then, pronouns should agree in number and gender with their antecedents. (In the sentences "Emilio washed their car" or "Emilio washed her car," you would assume a different car is being referred to.)

Singular: The student turned in her lab report.

Plural: The students turned in their lab reports.

Indefinite pronouns

Indefinite pronouns are those pronouns that don't refer to any specific person or thing such as "anyone," "no one," "someone," "something," "everybody," "none," and "each." Some of them may seem to have a plural meaning, but in formal writing, treat them as singular. Others, such as "many," are always plural, and "some" can be singular or plural depending on the meaning of the sentence.

When using indefinite pronouns that are normally treated as singular, some writers prefer to use the plural to avoid sexist language (section 10). But as an alternative, you can use "his or her" (which can be wordy) or switch to plural.

Everyone in the class took out his notebook.

Everyone in the class took out his or her notebook.

The students took out their notebooks.

Collective nouns

When you use collective nouns such as "committee," "family," "group," and "audience," treat them as singular because they are acting as a group.

The jury handed in its verdict.

Generic or general nouns

When you use generic nouns to indicate members of a group, such as "voter," "student," and "doctor," treat them as singular. To avoid sexist language, switch to plural.

A truck driver should keep his road maps close at hand.

Truck drivers should keep their road maps close at hand.

Pronoun reference

To avoid reader confusion, be sure your pronouns have a clear reference to their antecedents. Here are several possible problems to avoid:

Ambiguous pronoun reference

When a pronoun does not clearly indicate which of two or more possible antecedents it refers to, the reference is ambiguous. Rewrite the sentence to make sure the reference is clear.

Unclear reference: Marina told Michelle that she took
                              <u>her</u> bike to the library.
her = Marina?   her = Michelle?

*(Did Marina take Michelle's bike to the library, or did Ma-
rina take her own bike to the library?)*

Clear reference: When Marina took Michelle's bike to
                              the library, she told Michelle she was
                              borrowing it.

Vague pronoun reference ("this," "that," and "which")

When you use "this," "that," and "which" to refer to something, be sure the word refers to a specific antecedent that
has been named.

Vague pronoun reference: Ray worked in a national forest
                              last summer, and <u>this</u> may be
                              his career choice.
this = ?

*(What does "this" refer to? Because no word or phrase in
the first part of the sentence refers to the pronoun, the sentence needs to be revised so the antecedent is stated.)*

Clear pronoun reference: Ray worked in a national for-
                              est last summer, and <u>working
                              as a forest ranger</u> may be his
                              career choice.

Indefinite use of "you," "it," and "they"

Avoid the use of "you," "it," and "they" that doesn't refer to
any specific group.

Vague pronoun reference: Everyone knows <u>you</u> should
                              use sunscreen lotion when
                              out in bright summer sun.
you = ?

Clear pronoun reference: It is well known that <u>people</u>
                              should use sunscreen lotion
                              when out in bright summer sun.

Vague pronoun reference: In Hollywood <u>they</u> don't know
                              what type of <u>movies</u> the
                              American public wants to see.
they = ?

Clear pronoun reference: In Hollywood, <u>screenwriters
                              and producers</u> don't know
                              what type of movies the
                              American public wants to see.

15 Adjectives and Adverbs

Adjectives and adverbs are modifiers, but they modify different kinds of words:

Adjectives   ■ modify nouns and pronouns
             ■ answer the questions "which?" "how many?" and "what kind?"

<u>six</u> packages (how many? <u>six</u>)

<u>cheerful</u> smile (what kind? <u>cheerful</u>)

It is <u>cold</u>.

(An adjective after a linking verb modifies the subject and is called a "subject complement." Here, "cold" is an adjective modifying the subject pronoun "it.")

The water tastes <u>salty</u>. water = salty

(Some verbs, like "taste," "feel," "appear," and "smell," can be linking verbs.)

Adverbs   ■ modify verbs, verb forms, adjectives, and other adverbs
           ■ answer the questions "how?" "when?" "where?" and "to what extent?"
           ■ Most (but not all) adverbs end in *-ly*

danced <u>gracefully</u> (how? <u>gracefully</u>)

<u>very</u> long string (to what extent? <u>very</u>)

He ran ~~quick~~ quickly. (How did he run? <u>quickly</u>)

They sing ~~real~~ really loud. (How loud? <u>really</u>)

Adjectives	Adverbs
sure	surely
real	really
good	well
bad	badly

"Good," "bad," "badly," and "well"

The modifiers "good," "bad," "badly," and "well" can cause problems because they are occasionally misused in speech. In addition, "well" can function as an adjective or an adverb.

well (adjective) = healthy   well (adverb) = done satisfactorily

He played <u>well</u>. (*not* good)

Despite the surgery, I feel <u>well</u>. (*not* good)

The linebacker played <u>badly</u> today. (*not* bad)

She feels <u>bad</u> about missing that meeting. (*not* badly)

He looked <u>good</u> in that suit. (*not* well)

HINT

COMPLETING COMPARISONS

When you use adverbs such as "so," "such," and "too," be sure to complete the phrase or clause.

    that she laughed out loud
She is so happy.
      ^

             to ask for help
Tran's problem is that he is too proud.
                           ^

Comparatives and superlatives

Adjectives and adverbs are often used to show comparison, and the degree of comparison is indicated in their forms. Adjectives and adverbs with one or two syllables add *-er* and *-est* as endings, and longer adjectives and adverbs combine with the words "more" and "most" or "less" and "least."

■ **Positive** (when no comparison is made):

a <u>large</u> box   a <u>cheerful</u> smile

■ **Comparative** (when two things are compared):

the <u>larger</u> of the two boxes   a <u>more cheerful</u> smile

■ **Superlative** (when three or more things are compared):

the <u>largest</u> box   the <u>most cheerful</u> smile

REGULAR FORMS OF COMPARISON

Positive	Comparative	Superlative
(for one)	(for two)	(for three or more)
tall	taller	tallest
pretty	prettier	prettiest
selfish	more selfish	most selfish
unusual	more unusual	most unusual

IRREGULAR FORMS OF COMPARISON

Positive	Comparative	Superlative
(for one)	(for two)	(for three or more)
good	better	best
well	better	best
little	less	least
some	more	most
much	more	most
many	more	most
bad, badly	worse	worst

Absolute adjectives and adverbs

Some adjectives and adverbs such as "unique," "perfect," and "final" cannot logically be compared because there can't be degrees of being final or unique or perfect.

Terri has a ~~most~~ unique smile.

16 Modifiers

Dangling modifiers

A dangling modifier is a word or group of words that refers to (or modifies) a word or phrase that has not been clearly stated in the sentence. When an introductory phrase does not name the doer of the action, the phrase

is assumed to refer to the subject of the independent
clause that follows.

Having finished the assignment, Jeremy turned on the TV.

*("Jeremy," the subject of the independent clause, is the
doer of the action in the introductory phrase.)*

However, when the intended subject (or doer of the action)
of the introductory phrase is not stated, the result is a dangling modifier.

Having finished the assignment, the TV was turned on.

*(This sentence is not logical because it implies that the TV
finished the homework.)*

Dangling modifiers most frequently occur at the beginning of the sentence but can also appear at the end. They
often have an *-ing* verb or a "to" + verb phrase near the
start of the phrase. To repair a dangling modifier, name
the subject in the dangling phrase or as the subject of the
sentence.

Dangling: After completing a degree in education, more
experience in the classroom is also needed to
prepare a good teacher.

Revised: After completing a degree in education, good
teachers also need to gain more experience in
the classroom.

Dangling: To work as a lifeguard, practice in CPR is required.

Revised: To work as a lifeguard, applicants are required
to have practice in CPR.

Misplaced modifiers

Misplaced modifiers are words or groups of words placed so
far away from what is being referred to that the reader may
be confused.

Misplaced modifier: The assembly line workers were
told that they had been fired by the
personnel director.

*(Were the workers told by the personnel director that they
had been fired? Or were they told by someone else that the
personnel director had fired them?)*

Revised: The assembly line workers were told by the
                personnel director that they had been fired.

Misplaced modifiers are often the source of comedians' humor, as in the classic often used by Groucho Marx and others:

> The other day I shot an elephant in my pajamas. How he
> got in my pajamas I'll never know.

Single-word modifiers such as "only," "even," and "hardly"
should be placed immediately before the words they modify
or as close to that word as possible. Note the difference in
meaning in these two sentences:

> I earned nearly $50. (The amount was almost $50, but
> not quite.)

> I nearly earned $50. (I almost had the opportunity to earn
> $50, but it didn't work out.)

HINT

PLACING MODIFIERS CORRECTLY

Some one-word modifiers that may get misplaced:

almost	hardly	merely	only
even	just	nearly	simply

Split infinitives

Split infinitives occur when modifiers are inserted between
"to" and the verb. Some people object to split infinitives, but
others consider them grammatically acceptable when other
phrasing would be less natural.

> to <u>quickly</u> reach

> *(Here "quickly" fits naturally between the "to" and the
> verb "reach.")*

Some split infinitives such as "to more than double" are almost impossible to rephrase, so there is no modifier between "to" and the verb.

17 Shifts

To maintain consistency in writing, use the same perspective throughout a paper by maintaining the same person: first person ("I"), second person ("you"), and third person ("he," "she," "it," "one," or "they"). Maintain consistency in number, tense, and tone also.

Unnecessary shift in person: In a <u>person's</u> life, the most important
(3rd person)
thing <u>you</u> do is to decide on a career.
(2nd person)

Revised: In a <u>person's</u> life, the most important thing <u>he or she</u> does is to decide on a career.

Unnecessary shift in number: The working <u>woman</u> faces many
(singular)
challenges to advancement. When <u>they</u>
(plural)
marry and have children, <u>they</u> may need to take a leave of absence.

Revised: Working <u>women</u> face many challenges to advancement. When <u>they</u> marry and have children, <u>they</u> may need to take a leave of absence.

Keep writing with verbs in the same time (past, present, or future) unless the logic of what you are writing about requires a switch.

Unnecessary shift in tense: While we <u>were watching</u> the last game
(past)
of the World Series, the picture suddenly <u>gets</u> fuzzy.
(present)

Revised: While we <u>were watching</u> the last game of the World Series, the picture suddenly <u>got</u> fuzzy.

Once you choose a formal or informal tone for a paper, keep that tone consistent in your word choices. A sudden intrusion of a very formal word or phrase in an informal narrative or the use of slang or informal words in a formal report or essay indicate the writer's loss of control over tone.

Unnecessary shift in tone: The job of the welfare worker is to assist in a family's struggle to obtain funds for the <u>kids</u>' clothing and food.

("Kids" is a very informal word choice here for a sentence that is somewhat formal in tone.)

Revised: The job of the welfare worker is to assist in a family's struggle to obtain funds for the <u>children</u>'s clothing and food.

IV

Punctuation

This section includes the rules you'll need to use punctuation correctly.

continued ▶

Sentence Punctuation Patterns (for Commas, Semicolons, and Colons)

■ (Independent clause).

Everyone agreed to her suggestion.

■ (Independent clause), *for* (independent clause).
               and
               nor
               but
               or
               yet
               so (the coordinating conjunctions)

It took four years for the tree to produce a crop, but the fruit was abundant.

■ (Independent clause); (independent clause).

They arrived late; they offered no excuse.

■ (Independent clause); *thus*, (independent clause).
                    however,
                    nevertheless,
                    (or other independent clause markers)

They arrived late; however, they offered no excuse.

■ (Independent clause): (example, list of items, or explanation).

They needed three items: a contract, her signature, and payment.

He had only one fault: stupidity.

■ (Independent clause): (independent clause).

The candidate promised fewer taxes: he campaigned on a platform of eliminating property taxes.

■ *If* (dependent clause), (independent clause).
After
Because
Since
When
(or other dependent clause markers)

If he studies more, his grades will improve.

- (Independent clause) *if* (dependent clause).
    because
    since
    when
    after

    His grades will improve if he studies more.

- Subject, (nonessential dependent clause), verb/predicate.

    Mako, who is my cousin, is going to major in economics.

- Subject (essential dependent clause) verb/predicate.

    The movie that I rented last night was a box office failure.

 Commas

Commas between independent clauses

To use commas in independent clauses, you need to know the following:

> **Independent clause:** a clause that can stand alone as a sentence
> **Compound sentence:** a sentence with two or more independent clauses

When you join two or more independent clauses to make a compound sentence, use a comma and any of the seven joining words (coordinating conjunctions) listed here. Place a comma before the joining word. A compound sentence that does not have both the comma and the joining word is called a "comma splice" or "fused sentence." (See page 28.)

The seven joining words

For
And
Nor   Vanilla is my favorite ice cream, but chocolate is
But   a close second.
Or
Yet
So

(Some writers remember this list as "FAN BOYS," spelled out by the first letters of each word.)

Alternative: If the two independent clauses are very short, some writers leave out the comma.

It started raining but the game continued.

Alternative: If one of the independent clauses has a comma in it, use a semicolon instead as part of the joining pair.

Jillian, not Alesha, is captain of the team; but Alesha assists the coach during practices.

Commas after introductory word groups

If you include introductory words, phrases, or clauses before the main part of your sentence, place a comma after the introductory part to indicate the break.

Word: However, the farmer switched his crop to hay.
Phrase: Having lived in Korea, he enjoyed eating kimchee.
Clause: While I was working on my car, it started to rain.

Alternative: If the introductory element is short (no more than four or five words) and not likely to cause confusion, some writers leave out the comma. In the second example here, some readers might, at first, misread the sentence as stating that Matt was eating the cat, so a comma is needed.

In most cases the statistics were reliable.

While Matt ate, the cat watched intently.

Commas before and after nonessential elements

When you include words, phrases, or clauses that are not essential to the meaning of the sentence and could be included in another sentence instead, place commas before and after the nonessential element.

Dr. Gupta, who is a cardiac surgeon, retired after fifty years of practice.

Commas in series and lists

Use commas when you have three or more items in a series or list.

The painting was done in blues, greens, and reds.

Wherever Mr. Chaugh went in the town, whatever he saw, and whomever he met, he was reminded of his childhood days there.

HINT

ESSENTIAL AND NONESSENTIAL CLAUSES

You can decide if an element is essential by reading the sentence without it. If the meaning changes, that element is essential.

Essential:

Apples *that are green* are usually very tart.

   If you remove the phrase "that are green," the statement changes to indicate that all apples are usually very tart.

Nonessential:

Apples, *which are Bryna's favorite fruit,* are on sale this week at the market.

   Whether or not apples are Bryna's favorite fruit, they are still on sale this week at the market. Thus *which are Bryna's favorite fruit* is a nonessential element.

HINT

COMMAS WITH LISTS

Remember that there must be at least three items in a list in order to use commas. Some writers mistakenly put a comma between two items (often verbs) in a sentence:

   No one had ever been able to locate the source of the river, and follow all its tributaries.

Alternative: Although most writers prefer to use the comma before "and" in a list of three or more items, some writers omit it.

   The menu included omelets, pastas and salads.

Commas with adjectives

When you include two or more adjectives that describe a noun equally, separate the adjectives by commas. But not all adjectives describe a noun equally. A quick test to see if the adjectives are equal is to switch the order. If that still sounds correct to your ear, they're equal. Another test is to insert "and" between the adjectives.

happy, healthy child

(You can switch this to "healthy, happy child." You can also write "happy and healthy child.")

six large dogs

(You cannot switch this to "large six dogs" or "six and large dogs.")

Commas with interrupting words or phrases

Use commas to set off words and phrases that interrupt the sentence.

Louisa Marcos, a math teacher, won the award.

The committee was, however, unable to agree.

The weather prediction, much to our surprise, was accurate.

Commas with dates, addresses, geographical names, and numbers

■ With dates
   In a heading or list:

   February 25, 1999 (or) 25 February, 1999

   (No commas are needed to separate the day and month if the day is placed before the month.)

   In a sentence:

   The order was shipped on March 9, 1998, and not received until January 18, 1999.

■ With addresses
   In a letter heading or on an envelope:

   Michael Cavanaugh, Jr.
   1404 Danton Drive
   Mineola, NM 43723

   In a sentence:

   If you need more information, write to General Investment, 132 Maple Avenue, Martinsville, IL 60122.

■ With geographical names
   Put a comma after each item in a place name.

The conference next year will be in Chicago, Illinois, and in New Orleans, Louisiana, the year after that.

■ With numbers

8,190,434   27,000   1,300 (or) 1300

The herd included 9,200 head of cattle.

Commas with quotations

Use a comma after expressions such as "he said."

Everyone was relieved when the chairperson said, "I will table this motion until the next meeting."

Unnecessary commas

Don't separate a subject from its verb.
Unnecessary: Increasing numbers of eighteen-year-olds who vote are calling for stricter laws.

Don't put a comma between two verbs.
Unnecessary: We offered to lend her our notes and help her with the homework.

Don't put a comma before every "and" or "but."
Unnecessary: The automobile industry now designs fuel-efficient cars and is finding a large market for them.

Don't put a comma before a direct object, especially a clause that starts with "that."
Unnecessary: Shaundra explained to me that she was interested in hearing my view.

Don't put a comma before a dependent clause when it comes after an independent clause, except for extreme contrast.
Unnecessary: Deer populations are exploding because their natural enemies are disappearing.
But: He was delighted with the news, although he needed some time to absorb it.

Don't put a comma after "such as" or "especially."
Unnecessary: The take-out shop sold various soups, such as minestrone, bean, and chicken noodle.

 Apostrophes

Apostrophes with possessives

The apostrophe indicates a form of ownership, but this is not always obvious. To test for possession, turn the two words around into an "of the" phrase.

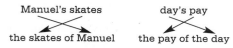

Manuel's skates   day's pay

the skates of Manuel   the pay of the day

■ For singular nouns, use **'s.**

   book**'s** cover   river**'s** edge

■ For singular nouns ending in **-s,** the **-s** after the apostrophe is optional if adding that **-s** makes the pronunciation difficult.

   Jame**'s** coat   (or)   James**'** coat
   Mr. Martinez**'** coat   grass**'s** color

■ For plural nouns ending in **-s,** add an apostrophe.

   books**'** covers   rivers**'** edges

■ For plural nouns that do not end in *-s,* use **-'s.**

   children**'s** toys   oxen**'s** tails

■ For possession with two or more nouns:

When jointly owned: Jim and Sabrina**'s** house

   (The house belongs jointly to both Jim and Sabrina.)

When individually owned: Jim**'s** and Sabrina**'s** plans

   (Jim and Sabrina each have their own plans.)

■ For compound nouns:

   sister-in-law**'s** car   secretary of state**'s** office

■ For indefinite pronouns (someone, everybody, etc.), use **-'s.**

   no one**'s** fault   somebody**'s** hat

Apostrophes with contractions

Use the apostrophe to mark the omitted letter or letters in contractions.

   it's = it is   don't = do not   they're = they are
   o'clock = of the clock   '89 = 1989

USING APOSTROPHES

When you aren't sure where the apostrophe goes, follow this order. Notice that everything to the left of the apostrophe is the word and its plural. Everything after the plural is the possessive marker.

1. Write the word.
2. Put in the plural if needed.
3. Put in the apostrophe for possession.

	Word	Plural	Possessive marker
girl's glove:	girl		-'s
girls' gloves	girl	-s	-'
men's gloves	men		-'s

Apostrophes with plurals

Use the apostrophe to form the plurals of letters, abbreviations with periods, numbers, and words used as words.

She got all A's last semester.

They all have Ph.D.'s.

He picked all 5's in the lottery.

Melissa's *maybe*'s were irritating.

Alternative: For some writers, the apostrophe is optional if the plural is clear.

9s	(or)	9's
1960s	(or)	1960's

But the apostrophe is needed here:

a's   A's

(Without the apostrophe, these might be the word "as.")

Unnecessary apostrophes

■ Don't use an apostrophe with possessive pronouns (his, hers, its, yours, whose, etc.).

his̶ arm   it̶'s edge   yours̶

■ Don't use an apostrophe with regular forms of plurals that
do not show possession.

The apple⃫s were ripe. They reduced the prices⃫.

21 Semicolons

The semicolon is a stronger mark of punctuation than the
comma, and it is used with two kinds of closely related elements:

1. between independent clauses
2. between items in a series.

It is almost like a period but does not come at the end of the
sentence.

Semicolons to separate independent clauses

Use a semicolon when joining two independent clauses (see
page 57) not joined by the seven connectors that require a
comma: *for, and, nor, but, or, yet,* and *so.*
Two patterns for using semicolons:

1. independent clause **+ semicolon** + independent clause

The television shots showed extensive flood damage**;**
houses were drifting downriver.

2. independent clause **+ semicolon + joining word +**
comma + independent clause

There was no warning before the flood**; however,** no lives
were lost.

Some frequently used joining words:

also,	finally,	instead,
besides,	for example,	on the contrary,
consequently,	however,	still,
even so,	in addition,	therefore,

Alternative: You can use a semicolon between two independent clauses joined with a coordinating conjunction
(section 19a) when one of those clauses has its own comma.
The semicolon makes the break between the two clauses
clearer.

The police officer, who was the first person on the scene, wrote down the information; and the newspaper relied on her account of the accident.

Semicolons in a series

Normally, commas are used between three or more items in a series (page 58), but when each item has its own comma, a semicolon can be used between items for clarity.

Luanne, Mina, and Karla

(or)

Luane, my first cousin; Mina, my best friend; and Karla, my neighbor

Semicolons with quotation marks

If a semicolon is needed, put it after the quotation marks.

Her answer to every question was, "I'll think about that"; she wasn't ready to make a decision.

Unnecessary semicolons

■ Don't use a semicolon between a clause and a phrase.

Mexico is my favorite vacation place; especially the
                              (should be a comma)
beaches in Cancun.

■ Don't use a semicolon in place of a dash, comma, or colon.

She spent the funds on a necessary piece of equipment for her home office; a computer.
                    (should be a colon)

 Quotation Marks

Quotation marks with direct quotations of prose, poetry, and dialogue

When you are writing the exact words you've seen in print or heard, use quotation marks when the quotation is less than four lines. For quotations that are four lines or longer, indent with no quotation marks.

Mrs. Alphonse said, "The test scores show improved reading ability."

In his poem, "Mending Wall," Robert Frost says: "Something there is that doesn't love a wall, / That sends the frozen-ground-swell under it."

(Notice the use of the slash to separate the two lines of poetry here.)

In his poem, "Mending Wall," Robert Frost questions the building of barriers and walls:

> Something there is that doesn't love a wall,
>
> That sends the frozen-ground-swell under it,
>
> And spills the upper boulders in the sun;
>
> And makes gaps even two can pass abreast.

■ If you have a quotation within a quotation, use single quotation marks (') to set off the quotation enclosed inside the longer quotation.

The newspaper reporter explained: "When I interviewed the lawyer, he said, 'No comment.'"

■ If you leave words out of a quotation, use an ellipsis mark (three periods; see page 73) to indicate the missing words.

The lawyer stated that he "would not . . . under any circumstances violate the client's desire for privacy."

■ If you add material within a quotation, use brackets [] (see page 72).

No one, explained the scientist, "could duplicate [Mayniew's] experiment without having his notes."

■ If you quote dialogue, write each person's speech as a separate paragraph. Closely related bits of narrative can be included with a paragraph with dialogue. If one person's speech goes on for several paragraphs, use quotation marks at the beginning of each paragraph, but not at the end of all paragraphs before the last one. To signal the end of the person's speech, put quotation marks at the end of the last paragraph.

Quotation marks for minor titles and parts of wholes

Use quotation marks for titles of parts of larger works (titles of book chapters, magazine articles, and episodes of television and radio series) and for short minor works (songs, short stories, essays, short poems, one-act plays). Do not use quotation marks when referring to the Bible or legal documents. For larger, more complete works, use italics (see page 80).

"The Star Spangled Banner"   Exodus 2:1
"Think Warm Thoughts" (an episode on *ER*)

Quotation marks for words

■ Use quotation marks (or italics) for words that are used as words rather than for their meaning.

It was tiresome to hear her always inserting "cool" or "like" in each sentence she spoke.

Use of other punctuation with quotation marks

■ Place commas and periods inside quotation marks. However, in MLA format, when you include a page reference, put the period after the page reference.

. . . was an advantage," she said.

. . . until tomorrow."

. . . when the eclipse occurs"(9).

■ Place colons and semicolons outside the quotation marks.

. . . until tomorrow": moreover, this will be . . .

■ Place the dash, exclamation mark, and question mark before the end set of quotation marks when the punctuation mark applies to the quotation. When the punctuation mark does not apply to the quotation, put the punctuation after the end set of quotation marks.

He asked, "Should I return the book to her?"

"Should I return the book to her?" he asked.

Did Professor Sandifur really say, "No class tomorrow"?

Unnecessary quotation marks

Don't use quotation marks around titles of your essays, common nicknames, bits of humor, technical terms, and trite or well-known expressions.

"Bubba" wanted the fastest "modem" available.

23 Other Punctuation

Hyphens

Hyphens have a variety of uses:

■ For compound words
   Some compound words are one word:

   weekend   mastermind   watercooler

   Some compound words are two words:

   high school   executive director   home run

   Some compound words are joined by hyphens:

   father-in-law   president-elect   clear-cut

   Fractions and numbers from twenty-one to ninety-nine
that are spelled out have hyphens.

   one-half   thirty-six   nine-tenths

   Particularly for new words or compounds that you are
forming, check your dictionary. You may find an answer
there, but not all hyphenated words appear there yet, especially new ones. Also, you will find that usage varies between dictionaries for some compounds.

   e-mail (or) email   witch-hunt (or) witch hunt

   wave-length (or) wavelength (or) wave length

   For hyphenated words in a series, use hyphens as
follows:

   four-, five-, and six-page essays

■ For two-word units
Use a hyphen when two or more words placed before a noun
work together as a single unit to describe the noun. When
these words come after the noun, they are usually not hyphenated. But don't use hyphens with adverbs such as -ly modifiers.

   He needed up-to-date statistics. (or) He needed statistics
   that were up to date.

   They repaired the six-inch pipe. (or) They repaired the
   pipe that was six inches long.

   That was a widely known fact.

   (not with adverbs such as those ending in -ly)

■ *For prefixes, suffixes, and letters joined to a word:*
Use hyphens between words and prefixes *self-*, *all-*, and *ex-*.

self-contained   all-American   ex-president

For other prefixes, such as *anti-*, *pro-*, and *co-*, use the dictionary as a guide.

co-author   antibacterial   pro-choice

Use a hyphen when joining a prefix to a capitalized word or to figures and numbers.

anti-American   non-Catholic   pre-1998

Use a hyphen when you add the suffix *-elect*.

president-elect

Use a hyphen to avoid doubling vowels and tripling consonants and to avoid ambiguity.

anti-intellectual   bell-like   re-creation

■ To divide words between syllables when the last part of the word appears on the next line.

Every spring the nation's capitol is flooded with tourists snapping pictures of the cherry blossoms.

When dividing words at the end of a line:

■ Don't divide one-syllable words.
■ Don't leave one or two letters at the end of a line.
■ Don't put fewer than three letters on the next line.
■ Don't divide the last word in a paragraph or the last word on a page.
■ Divide compound words so the hyphen for the compound comes at the end of the line. Or put the whole compound word on the next line.

Colons

Use colons as follows:

■ To announce elements at the end of the sentence

The company sold only electronics they could service: computers, stereos, CD players, and television sets.

■ To separate independent clauses
Use a colon instead of a semicolon to separate two independent clauses when the second restates or amplifies the first.

The town council voted not to pave the gravel roads outside of town: they did not have the funds for road improvement.

■ To announce long quotations

Use a colon to announce a long quotation (more than one sentence) or a quotation not introduced by words such as "said," "remarked," or "stated."

> The candidate for office offered only one reason to vote for her: "I will not raise parking meter rates."

■ In salutations and between elements

> Dear Dr. Philippa: 6:12 A.M.   Chicago: Howe Books
> Genesis 1:8   scale of 1:3   Maryland: My Home

■ With quotation marks

If a colon is needed, put it after the closing quotation mark.

> "One sign of intelligence is not arguing with your boss": that was her motto for office harmony.

■ Unnecessary colons

Do not use a colon after a verb or phrases like "such as" or "consisted of."

> The two most valuable players were Timon Lasmon and Maynor Field.

> The camping equipment consisted of tents, bug spray, lanterns, matches, and dehydrated food.

End punctuation

■ Periods

Use a period at the end of a sentence that is a statement, mild command, indirect question, or polite question where an answer isn't expected.

> Electric cars are growing in popularity. (statement)

> Do not use your calculator during the test. (mild command)

> Would you please let me know when you're done? (polite question)

Use a period with abbreviations, but don't use a second period if the abbreviation is at the end of the sentence.

> R.S.V.P.   U.S.A.   Dr.   Mr.   8 A.M.

A period is not needed after agencies, common abbreviations, names of well-known companies, and state abbreviations used by the U.S. Postal Service.

> NATO   NBA   IBM   DNA   TX

Put periods that follow quotations inside the quotation mark. But if there is a reference to a source, put the period after the reference.

She said, "I'm going to Alaska next week."

Neman notes "the claim is unfounded" (6).

■ Question marks
Use a question mark after a direct question but not after an indirect one.

Did anyone see my laptop computer? (direct question)

Jules wonders if he should buy a new stereo. (indirect question)

Place a question mark inside the quotation marks if the quotation is a question. Place the question mark outside the quotation marks if the whole sentence is a question.

Drora asked, "Is she on time?"

Did Eli really say, "I'm in love"?

Question marks may be used between parts of a series.

Would you like to see a movie? go shopping? eat at a restaurant?

Use a question mark to indicate doubt about the correctness of the preceding date, number, or other piece of information. But do not use it to indicate sarcasm.

The ship landed in Greenland about 1521 (?) but did not keep a record of where it was.

Matti's sense of humor (?) evaded me.

■ Exclamation marks
Use the exclamation mark after a strong command or a statement said with great emphasis or with strong feeling. But do not overuse the exclamation mark.

I'm absolutely delighted!

Unnecessary: Wow! What a great party! I enjoyed every minute of it!
Enclose the exclamation mark within the quotation marks only if it belongs to the quotation.

He threw open the door and exclaimed, "I've won the lottery!"

Dashes

The dash is somewhat informal but can be used to add emphasis or clarity, to mark an interruption or shift in tone, or to introduce a list. Use two hyphens to indicate the dash when you are typing, and do not leave a space before or after the hyphen.

> To be a millionaire, the owner of a yacht, and a race car driver—this was his goal.

> The cat looked at me so sweetly--with a dead rat in its mouth.

Slashes

Use the slash to mark the end of a line of poetry and to indicate acceptable alternatives. For poetry, leave a space before and after the slash. For alternatives, leave no space. The slash is also used in World Wide Web addresses.

> pass/fail   and/or

> He reiterated Milton's great lines: "The mind is its own place, and in itself / Can make a Heaven of Hell, a Hell of Heaven."

> http://www.whitehouse.gov

Parentheses

Use parentheses to enclose supplementary or less important material added as further explanation or example or to enclose figures or letters that enumerate a list.

> The newest officers of the club (those elected in May) were installed at the ceremony.

> They had three items on the agenda: (1) a revised budget, (2) the parking permits, and (3) a new election procedure.

Brackets

Use brackets to add your comments or additional explanation within a quotation and to replace parentheses within parentheses. The Latin word *sic* in brackets means you copied the original quotation exactly as it appeared, but you think there is an error there.

> We all agreed with Fellner's claim that "this great team [the Chicago Bears] is destined to go to the Super Bowl next year."

The lawyer explained, "We discussed the matter in a fiendly [*sic*] manner."

Omitted words/ellipsis

Use an ellipsis (a series of three spaced periods) to indicate that you are omitting words or part of a sentence from the source you are quoting. If you omit a whole sentence or paragraph, add a fourth period with no space after the last word preceding the ellipsis.

"modern methods . . . with no damage."

"the National Forest System . . ." (Smith 9).

"federal lands. . . . They were designated for preservation."

If you omit words immediately after a punctuation mark in the original, include that mark in your sentence.

"because of this use of the forest, . . ."

V

Mechanics

In this section are the rules for matters of mechanics, including capitalization, italics, numbers, abbreviations, and spelling.

continued ▶

24 Capitalization

Proper nouns vs. common nouns

Capitalize proper nouns, words that name one particular thing, most often a person or place rather than a general type or group of things.

Listed here are categories of words that should be capitalized. If you are not sure about a particular word, check your dictionary.

Proper noun	Common noun
James Joyce	man
Thanksgiving	holiday
University of Maine	state university
Macintosh	personal computer
May	spring

HINT: CAPITALIZING ACADEMIC SUBJECTS

Remember that general names of academic subjects, such as "history" or "economics," are not capitalized. However, the name of a specific department is capitalized: the History Department. (This proper noun describes a particular department. Another history department might be called the Department of Historical Studies.)

■ Persons

Caitlin Baglia   Hannah Kaplan   Masuto Tatami

■ Places, including geographical regions

Indianapolis   Ontario   Midwest

■ Peoples and their languages

Spanish   Dutch   English

■ Religions and their followers

Buddhist   Judaism   Christianity

■ Members of national, political, racial, social, civic, and athletic groups

Democrat	African American	Chicago Bears
Friends of the Library	Danes	Olympics Committee

■ Institutions and organizations

    Supreme Court   Legal Aid   Lions Club
                         Society

■ Historical documents

    Magna Carta   The Declaration of Independence

■ Periods and events (but not century numbers)

    Middle Ages   Boston Tea   eighteenth century
                         Party

■ Days, months, and holidays (but not seasons)

    Monday   Thanksgiving   winter

■ Trademarks

    Coca-Cola   Kodak   Ford

■ Holy books and words denoting the Supreme Being (including pronouns)

    Talmud   wonders of   the Bible
                     His creation

■ Words and abbreviations derived from specific names (but not the names of things that have lost the specific association and now refer to the general type)

    Stalinism   NATO   CBS
    french fry   pasteurize   italics

■ Place words ("City" or "Mountain") that are part of specific names

    New York City   Zion National   Wall Street
                      Park

■ Titles that precede people's names (but not titles that follow names)

    Aunt Sylvia   President Taft   Governor Sam Parma
    Sylvia, my aunt   Sam Parma, governor

■ Words that indicate family relationships when used as a substitute for a specific name

    Here is a gift for Mother.   She sent a gift to her mother.

■ Titles of books, magazines, essays, movies, and other works, but not articles ("a," "an," "the"), short prepositions ("to," "by," "on"), or short joining words ("and," "or") unless they are the first or last word. With hyphenated words, capitalize the first and other important words. (For APA style, which has different rules, see section 40.)

The Taming of the Shrew   "The Sino-Soviet Conflict"
A Dialogue Between Body and Soul   "My Brother-in-Law"

- The pronoun "I" and the interjection "O" (but not the word "oh")

  "Sail on, sail on, O ship of state," I said as the canoe sank.

- Words placed after a prefix that are normally capitalized

  un-American   anti-Semitic   ex-wife

Capitals in sentences, quotations, and lists

- Capitalize the first word in a sentence.
- Capitalize the first word of a sentence in parentheses but not when the parenthetical sentence is inserted within another sentence.
- Do not capitalize the first word in a series of questions in which the questions are not full sentences.

  What did the settlers want from the natives? food? horses?

- Capitalize the first word of directly quoted speech, but not for the second portion of interrupted direct quotations or quoted phrases or clauses integrated into the sentence.

  She answered, "No one will understand."

  "No one," she answered, "will understand."

  When Hemmings declined the nomination, he said that "this is not a gesture of support for the other candidate."

- The first word in a list after a colon if each item in the list is a complete sentence.

  The rule books were very clear: (1) No player could continue to play after committing two fouls. (2) Substitute players would be permitted only with the consent of the other team. (3) Every eligible player had to be designated before the game.

  (or)

  The rule books were very clear:

  1. No player could continue to play after committing two fouls.
  2. Substitute players would be permitted only with the consent of the other team.
  3. Every eligible player had to be designated before the game.

 **Italics**

When you are typing or writing by hand, use underlining (a printer's mark to indicate words to be set in italic type font) for those types of titles and names indicated here. If your computer has an italic font, use that instead of underlining.

italics type font = *italics*
underlining = underlining

Titles

Use italics for titles and names of long or complete works, including the following:

Books:	*Catcher in the Rye*
Magazines:	*Time*
Newspapers:	*The New York Times*
Works of art (visual and performance):	*Swan Lake*
Pamphlets:	*Coping with Diabetes*
Television and radio series (not titles of individual episodes):	*Sixty Minutes*
Films and videos:	*Titanic*
Long plays:	*Macbeth*
Long musical works:	*Symphony in B Minor*
Long poems:	*Paradise Lost*
Software:	*PageMaker*
Recordings:	*Yellow Submarine*

■ Do not italicize or use quotation marks for the Bible and other major religious works or for legal documents.

Koran   The Constitution   Bible

■ For shorter works or parts of whole works, use quotation marks (see section 22).

Other uses of italics/underlining

■ Names of ships, airplanes, and trains

Queen Mary   *Concorde*   *Orient Express*

■ Foreign words and scientific names of plants and animals

in vino veritas   *Canis lupis*

■ Words used as words or letters, numbers, and symbols used as examples or terms

Some words, such as *Kleenex,* are brand names.

The letters *ph* and *f* often have the same sound.

■ Words being emphasized

It *never* snows here in April.

(Use italics or underlining for emphasis only sparingly.)

Do not use italics or underlining for the following:

■ Words of foreign origin that are now part of English:
alumni   karate   hacienda

■ Titles of your own papers

26 Numbers

Style manuals for different fields and companies vary. The suggestions for writing numbers offered here are generally useful as a guide for academic writing.

■ Spell out numbers that can be expressed in one or two words and use figures for other numbers.

Words	Figures
two pounds	126 days
six million dollars	$31.95
thirty-one years	6.381 bushels
eighty-three people	4.6 liters

■ When you write several numbers, be consistent in choosing words or figures.

He didn't know whether to buy ~~nine~~ gallons of milk or 125 separate small containers.

■ Use figures for the following:

Days and years

December 12, 1921	(or)	12 December 1921
in 1971–72	(or)	in 1971–1972
the 1990's	(or)	the 1990s
A.D. 1066		

Time of day

8 p.m. (or) P.M.	(or)	eight o'clock in the evening
2:30 a.m. (or) A.M.	(or)	half past two in the morning

Addresses
15 Tenth Avenue
350 West 114 Street   (or)   350 West 114th Street
Prescott, AZ 86301

Identification numbers
Room 8   Channel 18
Interstate 65   Henry VIII

Page and division of books and plays
page 30   chapter 6
act 3, scene 2   (or)   Act III, Scene ii

Decimals and percentages
2.7 average   12 and 1/2 percent
0.036 metric ton

Numbers in series and statistics
two apples, six oranges, and three bananas
115 feet by 90 feet

(Be consistent whichever form you choose.)

Large round numbers
four billion dollars   (or) $4 billion
16,500,000   (or)   16.5 million

Repeated numbers (in legal or commercial writing)
The bill will not exceed one hundred (100) dollars.

■ Do not use figures for the following:

Numbers that can be expressed in one or two words
the eighties   the twentieth century

Dates when the year is omitted
June sixth   May fourteenth

Numbers beginning a sentence
Ten percent of the year's crop was harvested.

 **Abbreviations**

In the fields of social science, science, and engineering, abbreviations are used frequently. But in other fields and in academic writing in the humanities, only a limited number of abbreviations are generally used.

Abbreviating titles

■ "Mr.," "Mrs.," and "Ms." are abbreviated when used as titles before the name.

Mr. Tanato   Ms. Ojebwa

■ "Dr." and "St." ("Saint") are abbreviated only when they immediately precede a name; they are written out when they appear after the name.

Dr. Martin Klein (but) Martin Klein, doctor of pediatrics

■ "Prof.," "Sen.," "Gen.," "Capt.," and similar abbreviated titles can be used when they appear in front of a name or before initials and a last name. But they are not abbreviated when they appear with the last name only.

Gen. R.G. Fuller   (but)   General Fuller

■ "Sr.," "Jr.," "Ph.D.," "M.F.A.," "C.P.A.," and other abbreviated academic titles and professional degrees can be used after the name.

Lisle Millen, Ph.D.   Charleen Dyer, C.P.A.

■ "Bros.," "Co.," and similar abbreviations are used only if they are part of the exact name.

Marshall Field & Co.   Brown Bros.

Abbreviating places

In general, spell out names of states, countries, continents, streets, rivers, and so on. But there are several exceptions:

■ Use the abbreviation "D.C." in Washington, D.C.
■ Use "U.S." only as an adjective, not as a noun.

U.S. training bases   training bases in the United States

■ If you include a full address in a sentence, citing the street, city, and state, you can use the postal abbreviation for the state.

For further information, write to the company at 100 Peachtree Street, Atlanta, GA 30300 for a copy of their catalog.

(but)

The company's headquarters in Atlanta, Georgia, will soon be moved.

Abbreviating numbers

■ Write out numbers that can be expressed in one or two words.

  twenty-seven   135

■ The dollar sign abbreviation is generally acceptable when the whole phrase will be more than three words.

  $36 million   one million dollars

■ For temperatures, use words if only a few temperatures are cited, but use figures if temperatures are cited frequently in a paper.

  ten degrees below zero, Fahrenheit   −10°F

Abbreviating measurements

Spell out units of measurement, such as acre, meter, foot, and percent, but use abbreviations in tables, graphs, and figures.

Abbreviating dates

Spell out months and days of the week. With dates and times, the following are acceptable:

  57 A.D. (or) 57 B.C.E. (Before the Common Era)
  A.D. 329 (The abbreviation A.D. is placed before the date.)
  a.m., p.m. (or) A.M., P.M.
  EST (or) E.S.T., est

Abbreviating names of familiar organizations and other entities

Use abbreviations for names of organizations, agencies, countries, and things usually referred to by their capitalized initials.

  NASA   IBM   VCR   AFL-CIO
  UNICEF   USSR   CNN   YMCA

If an abbreviation may not be familiar to your readers, spell out the term the first time you use it, with the abbreviation in parentheses. From then on, you can use the abbreviation.

  The Myer-Briggs Type Inventory (MBTI) is offered in the dean's Career Counseling Office. Students who take the MBTI can then speak to a career counselor about the results.

Abbreviating Latin expressions and documentation terms

Some Latin expressions always appear as abbreviations:

Abbreviation	Meaning
cf.	compare
e.g.	for example
et al.	and others
etc.	and so forth
vs. (or) v.	versus
N.B.	note well

These abbreviations are appropriate for bibliographies and footnotes, as well as in informal writing, but for formal writing, use the English phrase instead.

Because the format for abbreviations in documentation may vary from one style manual to another, use the abbreviations listed in the particular style manual you are following. (See, for example, the suggestions for MLA and APA in sections 39–40.)

Abbreviation	Meaning
abr.	abridged
anon.	anonymous
ed., eds.	editor, editors
p., pp.	page, pages
vol., vols.	volume, volumes

 **28 Spelling**

English spelling is difficult because it contains so many words from other languages that have different spelling conventions. In addition, unlike some other languages that have only one spelling for a sound, English has several ways to spell some sounds. But it's important to spell correctly, to be sure your reader understands your writing. Also, misspelled words can signal to the reader that the writer is careless and not very knowledgeable.

Because no writer wants to lose credibility, correct spelling is necessary. The following suggestions should help ensure that your papers are spelled correctly:

■ Learn some spelling rules.

See the following pages for some useful rules.

■ Learn your own misspelling patterns and troublesome words.

When you identify a word that tends to cause you problems, write it down in a list and if possible, make up your own memory aid. For example, if you can't remember whether "dessert" is that barren sandy place like the Mohave (or Sahara) or the sweet treat you eat after a meal, try making up some rule or statement that will stick in your mind. For "dessert" and "desert," you might try a reminder such as the fact that the word for the sweet treat has two *s*'s, and you like seconds on desserts.

■ Use a spell checker.

Spell checkers are helpful tools, but they can't catch all spelling errors. Although different spell checking programs have different capabilities, they are not foolproof, and they do make mistakes. Most spell checkers do not catch the following types of errors:

1. **Omitted words**
2. **Sound-alike words (homonyms)**
   Some words sound alike but are spelled differently. For example, the spell checker cannot distinguish between "there" and "their."
3. **Substitution of one word for another**
   If you meant to write "one" and typed "own" instead, the spell checker will not flag that.
4. **Proper nouns**
   Some well-known proper nouns, such as "Washington," may be in the spell checker, but many will not be.
5. **Misspelled words**
   If you have misspelled a word, the spell checker may be able to suggest the correct spelling. But for other misspellings, the spell checker will not be able to offer the correct spelling. You will need to know how to use a dictionary to look it up.

■ Learn how to proofread.

Proofreading requires slow and careful reading to catch misspellings and typographical errors. This is hard to do because we are used to reading quickly and seeing a group of words together. Some useful proofreading strategies are the following:

1. **Slow down.** For best results, slow down your reading rate so you actually see each word.
2. **Focus on each word.** One way to slow down is to point a pencil or pen at each word as you say it aloud or to

yourself. Note with a check in the margin any word
that doesn't look quite right, and come back to it later.

3. **Read backward.** Don't read right to left, as you usually
do, or you will soon slip back into a more rapid reading
rate. Instead, move backward through each line from
right to left. In this way, you won't be listening for
meaning or checking for grammatical errors.

4. **Cover up distractions.** To focus on each word, hold a
sheet of paper or a note card under the line being
read. That way you won't be distracted by other
words on the page.

Some spelling guidelines

1. ie/ei

> Write *i* before *e*
> Except after *c*
> Or when sounded like "ay"
> As in "neighbor" or "weigh."

This rhyme reminds you to write *ie,* except under two conditions:

■ When the two letters follow a *c*
■ When the two letters sound like "ay" (as in "day")

Some *ie* words		Some *ei* words	
believe	niece	ceiling	eight
chief	relief	conceit	receive
field	yield	deceive	vein

Some exceptions to this rule:

conscience	foreign	neither	species
counterfeit	height	science	sufficient
either	leisure	seize	weird

2. Doubling consonants

One-syllable words
If the word ends in a single short vowel and then a consonant, double the last consonant when you add a suffix
beginning with a vowel.

drag	dragged	dragging
star	starred	starring
tap	tapped	tapping
wet	wetted	wetting

Two-syllable words

If the word has two or more syllables and then a single vowel and a consonant, double the consonant when (1) you are adding a suffix that begins with a vowel, and (2) the last syllable of the base word is accented.

begin		beginning
occur	occurred	occurring
omit	omitted	omitting
prefer	preferred	preferring
refer	referred	referring

3. Final silent -*e*

Drop the final silent -*e* when you add a suffix beginning with a vowel.

line	lining
smile	smiling

But keep the final -*e* when the suffix begins with a consonant.

care	careful
like	likely

Words such as "true/truly" and "argue/argument" are exceptions to this.

4. Plurals

Generally, most words add -*s* for plurals. But add -*es* when the word ends in -*s*, -*sh*, -*ch*, -*x*, or -*z* because another syllable is needed.

one apple	two apples
one box	two boxes
a brush	some brushes

With phrases and hyphenated words, pluralize the last word unless another word is more important.

one videocassette recorder	two videocassette recorders
one sister-in-law	two sisters-in-law

For words ending in a consonant plus -*y*, change the -*y* to -*i* and add -*es*. For proper nouns, keep the -*y*.

one boy	two boys
one company	two companies
Mr. Henry	the Henrys

HINT

AVOIDING WRONG APOSTROPHES

Some writers mistakenly add an apostrophe for plurals.

one book   two books

a monkey   the cage of monkeys

For some words, the plural is formed by changing the base word. Some other words have the same form for singular and plural. And other words, taken from other languages, form the plural in the same way as the original language.

one child	two children
one woman	two women
one deer	two deer
one datum	much data
one medium	many media
a phenomenon	some phenomena

Sound-alike words (homonyms)

accept:	to agree/receive	accept a gift
except:	other than	all except her
affect:	to influence	Insomnia affects me.
effect:	a result	What was the effect?
hear:	(verb)	Did you hear that?
here:	indicates a place	Come here.
its:	shows possession	Its leg is broken.
it's:	= it is	It's raining out.
quiet:	no noise	Be quiet!
quite:	very	That's quite nice.
quit:	give up	He quit his job.
than:	used to compare	taller than I
then:	time word	Then he went home.
to:	preposition	to the house
too:	also	She is too tired to work.

were:	verb	were singing
we're:	= we are	We're going on vacation.
where:	in what place	Where is he?
who's:	= who is	Who's going to the movies?
whose:	shows possession	Whose book is this?
your:	shows possession	What is your name?
you're:	= you are	You're right!

VI

Multilingual Speakers (ESL)

This section includes topics that are especially useful for students whose first language is not English.

continued ▶

- Which is the correct preposition?

- Why are the following sentences not correct?

- Some phrases in English do not mean exactly what the words mean (such as "dead as a doornail"). How do I learn what these mean?

29 American Style in Writing

If your first language is not English, you may have some writing style preferences and some questions about English grammar and usage. Some of these matters are addressed in this section, and if you have individual questions and are a student at an institution with a writing center, talk with a tutor in the writing center.

Your style preferences and customs will depend on what language(s) you are more familiar with, but in general, consider the following differences between the language(s) you know and academic style in American English. Academic style in American English is characterized by the following:

Conciseness

In some languages, writers strive for a type of eloquence marked by a profusion of words and phrases that elaborate on the same topic. Effective academic style in American English, however, is concise, eliminating extra or unnecessary words.

Clearly announced topic at the beginning of the paper

In some languages, the topic is delayed or not immediately announced. Instead, suggestions lead readers to formulate the main ideas for themselves. In American English, there is a decided preference for announcing the topic in the opening paragraph or somewhere near the beginning of the paper.

Tight organization

Although digressions into side topics or related matters can be interesting and are expected in writing in some languages, American academic writing stays on topic and does not digress.

Sources are clearly cited

In some languages, less attention is paid to citing sources of information, ideas, or the exact words used by others. In American academic writing, however, writers are expected to cite all sources other than what is generally known by most people. Otherwise, the writer is in danger of being viewed as plagiarizing.

When you are considering matters of grammar and usage, the following are topics that may cause difficulty as you write in English.

30 Verbs

Unlike some other languages, verbs are required in English sentences. Verbs are very important parts of English sentences because they indicate time and person (see section 13).

Verb tenses

Progressive tenses: use a form of "be" plus *-ing* form of the verb such as "going" or "running."

She is going to the concert tonight.

Perfect tenses: use a form of "have" plus the past participle, such as "walked" or "gone."

1. Present tense

■ Simple present

presents action or condition

They <u>ride</u> their bikes.

general or literary truth

States <u>defend</u> their rights.

Shakespeare <u>uses</u> humor effectively.

habitual action

I <u>like</u> orange juice for breakfast.

future time

The plane <u>arrives</u> at 10 P.M. tonight.

■ Present progressive

activity in progress, not finished, or continued

I <u>am majoring</u> in engineering.

■ Present perfect

action that began in the past and leads up to and continues into the present

He <u>has worked</u> here since May.

■ Present perfect progressive

action begun in the past, continues to the present, and may continue into the future

I <u>have been thinking</u> about buying a car.

2. Past tense

■ Simple past

completed action or condition

She <u>walked</u> to class.

■ Past progressive

past action over a period of time or that was interrupted by another action

The engine <u>was running</u> while he waited.

■ *Past perfect*

action or event completed before another event in the past

He <u>had</u> already <u>left</u> when I arrived.

■ *Past perfect progressive*

ongoing condition in the past that has ended

She <u>had been speaking</u> to that group.

3. Future tense

■ Simple

actions or events in the future

They <u>will arrive</u> tomorrow.

■ Future progressive

future action that will continue for some time

I <u>will be expecting</u> you.

■ Future perfect

actions that will be completed by or before a specified time in the future

By Monday, <u>I will have cleaned up</u> that cabinet.

■ Future perfect progressive

ongoing actions or conditions until a specified time in the future

She <u>will have been traveling</u> for six months by the time she arrives here.

Helping verbs with main verbs

Helping (or auxiliary) verbs combine with other verbs. (See section 13.)

be: "be," "am," "is," "are," "was," "were," "being," "been"
do: "do," "does," "did"
have: "have," "has," "had"
modals: "can," "could," "may," "might," "must," "shall," "should," "will," "would," "ought to"

Modal verbs are helping verbs that indicate possibility, uncertainty, necessity, or advisability. Use the base form of the verb after a modal.

May I ask you a question?

Two-word (phrasal) verbs

Some verbs are followed by a second (and sometimes a third) word that combine to indicate the meaning. Many dictionaries indicate the meanings of these phrasal verbs.

look over (examine):	She looked over the contract.
look up (search):	I will look up his phone number.
look out for (watch for):	Look out for the puddle.

The second word of some of these verbs can be separated from the main verb by a noun or pronoun:

add (it) up   put (the phone call) off

In other cases, the second word cannot be separated from the main verb:

back out of the garage   get through the mob

Verbs with *-ing* and with "to" + verb form

Some verbs combine only with the *-ing* form of the verb; some verbs combine only with the "to" + verb form (the infinitive form); some verbs can be followed by either form.

Verbs followed only by *-ing* forms

admit	enjoy	recall
appreciate	finish	regret
deny	keep	stop
dislike	practice	suggest

He admits spending that money.

Verbs followed only by "to" + verb

agree	have	plan
ask	mean	promise
claim	need	wait
decide	offer	want

She <u>needs to take</u> that medicine.

Verbs that can be followed by either form

begin	intend	prefer
continue	like	start
hate	love	try

They <u>begin to sing</u>. (or) They <u>begin singing</u>.

 Nouns (Count and Noncount)

Nouns are either proper nouns that name specific things and begin with capital letters (see section 24) or common nouns. There are two kinds of common nouns, those that can be counted (count nouns) and those that cannot be counted (noncount nouns).

1. **Count nouns:** name things that can be counted because those things can be divided into separate and distinct units. Count nouns have plurals and usually refer to things that can be seen, heard, touched, tasted, or smelled.

one apple	some apples
a chair	six chairs
the child	all of the children

2. **Noncount nouns:** name things that cannot be counted because they are abstractions or things that cannot be cut into parts. Noncount nouns do not have plurals, do not have "a" or "an" preceding them, and may have a collective meaning.

air	humor	oil	weather
furniture	money	beauty	clothing

   To indicate amounts for noncount nouns, use a count noun that quantifies:

a pound of coffee	a loaf of bread
a quart of milk	a great deal of money

HINT

NONCOUNT NOUNS

Many foods are noncount nouns:

coffee	tea	corn	water
cereal	milk	candy	flour

32 Articles ("A," "An," and "The")

A/An

"A" and "an" identify nouns in a general or indefinite way and refer to any member of a group. "A" and "an" are generally used with singular count nouns.

Please hand me a towel.

(This sentence does not specify which towel, just any towel that is handy.)

The

"The" identifies a particular or specific noun in a group or a noun already specified in a previous phrase or sentence. "The" may be used with singular or plural nouns.

Please hand me the towel that is on the table.

(This sentence means that not just any towel is being requested—only the one particular towel that is on the table.)

A new computer model is being introduced. The new model will probably cost more.

("A" is used first in a general way to mention the model, and then, because it has been specified, it is referred to as "the" model.)

Some uses of "the."

■ Use "the" when an essential phrase or clause follows the noun.

The man who addressed the group is my art teacher.

■ Use "the" when the noun refers to a class as a whole.

He explained that the fox is a nocturnal animal.

■ Use "the" with names composed partly of common nouns and plural nouns.

the British Commonwealth   the United States
the Netherlands   the University of Illinois

■ Use "the" with names that refer to rivers, oceans, seas, deserts, forests, gulfs, and peninsulas and with points of the compass used as names.

the Nile   the Persian Gulf   the South

■ Use "the" with superlatives

the best reporter   the most expensive car

No articles

Articles are not used with names of streets, cities, states, countries, continents, lakes, parks, mountains, names of languages, sports, holidays, universities, and academic subjects.

He traveled to Africa.   She is studying Chinese.
He likes to watch tennis.   He graduated from Brandeis.

 **33** **Prepositions**

Prepositions in English show relationships between words and are difficult to master because they are idiomatic. The following lists some of the most commonly used prepositions and the relationships they indicate.

Prepositions of time

On   used with days

on Monday

At   used with hours of the day

at 9 A.M.

In   used with other parts of the day

in the afternoon

Prepositions of place

On   indicates a surface on which something rests

           The car was parked <u>on</u> the street.

At   indicates a point in relation to another subject

           My sister is <u>at</u> home.

In   indicates a subject is inside the boundaries of an
           area or volume

           The sample is <u>in</u> the bottle.

Prepositions to show logical relationships

Of   shows relationship between a part and the whole

           Two <u>of</u> her teachers gave quizzes today.

           shows material or content

           That basket <u>of</u> fruit is a present.

For   shows purpose

           He bought some plants <u>for</u> the garden.

34 Omitted/Repeated Words

Omitted words

Subjects and verbs can be omitted in some languages, but
they are necessary in English sentences and must appear.
The only exception in English is the command that has an
understood subject: "Put that box here." (The understood
subject here is "you.")

Subjects

Include a subject in the main clause and in all other clauses as
well. "There" and "it" may sometimes serve as subject words.

All the children laughed while _{they} were watching cartoons.

It i

Is raining today.

Verbs

Although verbs such as "is" and "are" and helping verbs can be omitted in some languages, they must appear in English.

is

She ∧ an effective Spanish teacher.

had

No one ∧ gone to the lecture.

Repeated words

In some languages, the subject can be repeated as a pronoun before the verb. However, in English, the subject is included only once.

Bones in the body ~~they~~ become brittle as people grow older.

In some languages, objects of verbs or prepositional phrases are repeated, but not in English.

The woman tried on the hat that I left ~~it~~ on the seat.

The city where I live ~~there~~ has two soccer fields.

 **Idioms**

An idiom is an expression that means something beyond the simple definition or literal translation into another language. An idiom such as "kick the bucket" (meaning "die") is not understandable from the meanings of the individual words.

Dictionaries of American English idioms can define many of the commonly used ones. The second word in two-word verb phrases (phrasals; see section 30) is idiomatic and changes meanings.

dark horse = someone not likely to be the winner
under the table = something done illegally
to turn <u>off</u> the light = to shut the light, to stop it
to set an <u>alarm</u> to go <u>off</u> = to make an alarm work, to start it

VII

Research

This section covers the process of doing research, from finding and narrowing a topic to evaluating and collecting information, and it includes some useful sources for finding relevant material. It also discusses summaries, paraphrases, and quotations and suggestions for integrating them into your paper, as well as plagiarism and how to avoid it.

continued ▶

36 Doing Research

Some research papers that present your findings on a topic may be objective and discuss only the information you found but not your opinion or perspective on the topic. Other research papers may be persuasive because after presenting the information you found, you come to conclusions or argue your opinion or viewpoint. Be sure that you know which one is the appropriate goal as you write the paper.

Doing research is a process of selecting a topic, formulating the research question(s) you will address, searching for information, taking notes and keeping a list of the citations, evaluating what you have found, organizing the material, writing the paper, including adequate support for your thesis, and citing your sources.

Selecting a topic

There are four steps to selecting a topic:

1. **Find** a general subject that interests you (if one has not been assigned). One way to locate an interesting subject is to browse through any book or catalog of subject headings such as the *Library of Congress Subject Headings* or the *Reader's Guide to Periodical Literature.* On the Web, you can browse through subject directories (see section 40 for specific sites to try). You can also browse through journals in a field you are interested in to look at topics discussed there. (See page 108 for a resource list of journals you are likely to find in your library.) For example:

   ■ Imagery in Maya Angelou's poetry

   ■ Careers in technical writing

2. **Narrow** that subject to a topic to fit the assignment and the length of the paper you will write. To narrow a topic, begin by listing some subtopics or smaller aspects of the larger topic, and choose one of those subtopics.

   ■ Maya Angelou's use of fire imagery

   ■ Technical writing jobs in the computer industry

3. **Formulate a research question** about your topic. Your research question will help you decide what information is relevant. Try formulating the question with any of the reporter's "who," "what," "where," "why," "when," and "how" questions.

- How does Maya Angelou use fire imagery in her poetry?

- What kinds of jobs are available in the computer industry for technical writing majors?

4. **Formulate a thesis statement** that answers your research question. After completing your research and reviewing your information, you will be able to formulate a tentative thesis. This statement will answer your research question, but it may need to be revised somewhat as you write your paper.

- Maya Angelou uses images of fire in her poetry to convey cleansing and rebirth.

- In the computer industry, technical writing majors are hired to write documents such as computer manuals, training materials, and in-house newsletters.

Finding information

The two categories of information to use are primary and secondary sources:

1. Primary sources

Primary sources are original or firsthand materials such as the poem or novel by the author you are writing about. Other primary materials are surveys, speeches, interviews you conduct, or firsthand accounts of events. Primary sources are not filtered through a second person. They may be more accurate because they have not been distorted or misinterpreted.

2. Secondary sources

Secondary sources are secondhand accounts, information, or reports about primary sources. Typical secondary sources include

HINT

ESL HINT: STATING YOUR IDEAS

Although some cultures place more value on student writing that primarily brings together or collects the thoughts of great scholars or experts, readers of research papers in American institutions value the writer's own interpretations and thinking about the subject.

reviews, biographies about a person you are studying, documentaries, encyclopedia articles, and other materials interpreted or studied by others. Remember that secondary sources are interpretations or analyses that may be biased, inaccurate, or incomplete.

Sources of information

1. *Libraries*

   Libraries have various printed guides for users and an information desk where you can talk with helpful librarians. In addition to the catalogs, some other indexes, catalogs, and databases you can browse through include the following:

   ■ *Books in Print*
   ■ *Reader's Guide to Periodical Literature*
   ■ Encyclopedias such as *Collier's Encyclopedia* and more specialized ones such as the *Harvard Guide to American History* and the *Oxford Companion to English Literature*
   ■ Abstracts and almanacs such as *Statistical Abstracts of the United States*
   ■ Online searches of the library's holdings by author, title, keyword, and subject heading
   ■ *Library of Congress Subject Headings* (This is helpful for subject heading searches when working online and can suggest alternate ways of phrasing keywords for your topic.)
   ■ Electronic databases such as the following:
   Business and Industry
   Business Periodicals Index
   CINAHL: Cumulative Index to Nursing and Allied
      Health Literature
   Contemporary Authors
   Contemporary Literary Criticism Select
   Dictionary of Literary Biography
   ERIC
   GPO Index
   Humanities Index
   Literary Resource Center
   MathSciNet
   MedLine
   Newspaper Source
   PsycINFO
   Social Science Index
   ■ Computerized bibliographic utilities such as *First-Search* (that accesses databases such as academic

journals, corporations, congressional publications, and medical journals) or *Newsbank CD News* (that indexes articles from a variety of newspapers). Nexis/Lexis is a commercial service available online and has abstracts and full texts of magazines, newspapers, publications from industry and government, wire services, and other sources.

2. *The Internet*

   See section 39 for a discussion of finding information on the Internet (page 125), searching useful sites (section 40), evaluating resources you find there (section 41), and citing Internet sources (section 42). Formats listed for MLA, APA, and others are in sections 43, 44, and 45.

3. *Community sources*

   Your community has a variety of resources to tap, including public records and other local government information in a city hall or county courthouse. Other sources are community service workers, social service agencies, schoolteachers and school administrators, community leaders, religious leaders, coordinators in nonprofit groups, the local chamber of commerce or visitors and convention bureau, local public library, museums or historical societies, the newspaper, and your campus offices and faculty.

4. *Interviews and surveys*

   You can do field research by interviewing people, sending e-mail messages, conducting surveys, and taking notes on your own observations.

Sources in various disciplines

When you are seeking information in various fields of study, the following lists of journals should help you. Also, check the Web sites listed in section 40 (Web Resources).

RESEARCH SOURCES IN VARIOUS FIELDS: JOURNALS AND MAGAZINES

Art	■ *American Artist*	■ *Art History*
	■ *Artforum*	■ *Metropolis*
Biology	■ *JAMA: Journal of the American Medical Association*	
	■ *Quarterly Review of Biology*	

Business/Economics/Management
- *Business Week*
- *Economist*
- *Harvard Business Review*
- *Journal of Business*
- *Sloan Management Review*

Communication
- *Communication Monographs*
- *Journalism & Mass Communication*
- *Quarterly Journal of Speech*

Composition and Rhetoric
- *College Composition and Communication*
- *College English*

Computer Science
- *Artificial Intelligence*
- *Byte*
- *Harvard Computer Review*
- *Technical Computing*

Culture
- *Common Knowledge*
- *Language, Society, and Culture*

Education
- *Education Research and Perspectives*
- *Education Week*

Engineering
- *Space Technology*
- *Automotive Engineering*
- *Industrial Engineering*

Environment
- *Amicus*
- *Atmospheric Environment*
- *Center for Health and the Global Environment Newsletter*
- *The Earth Times*
- *Environmental Health Perspectives Journals*

History
- *American Historical Review*
- *American History*
- *English Literary History*
- *History Today*
- *Journal of Social History*
- *Journal of Modern History*
- *Journal of World History*

Law	■ *IDEA: The Journal of Law and Technology*
	■ *Intellectual Property*
	■ *Journal of Information Law and Technology*

Literature	■ *African-American Review*
	■ *Journal of Modern Literature*
	■ *PMLA*

| Movies | ■ *KINEMA: A Journal for Film and Audiovisual Media* |

| Music | ■ *Journal of Musicology* |
| | ■ *Musical Quarterly* |

| Physics | ■ *Physical Review* |
| | ■ *Physics Letters* |

Political Science
- ■ *The Americana*
- ■ *Congressional Quarterly*
- ■ *Foreign Affairs*
- ■ *Harvard Political Review*
- ■ *Political Science Quarterly*
- ■ *Yale Political Monthly*

Psychology	■ *American Journal of Psychology*
	■ *Counseling Psychologist*
	■ *Journal of Personality and Social Psychology*
	■ *Psychological Review*

| Religion | ■ *Cross Currents* |
| | ■ *Religion and Literature* |

Sociology	■ *American Sociological Review*
	■ *Human Development and Family Life*
	■ *Journal of Sociology and Social Welfare*

Women's Studies
- ■ *Journal of Women's History*
- ■ *Sister*
- ■ *Womanist Theory and Research*
- ■ *Women's Review of Books*

Taking notes

Working bibliography

As you collect information, start a working bibliography that lists all the sources you will read. See section 37 on evaluating the citation before you spend time locating it. Some sources won't be as useful, and there are some questions you can ask yourself as you look at citations to see whether they belong in your working bibliography.

Because you may not use all those sources in your paper, the final list of sources is likely to be shorter than the working bibliography. Make bibliographic entries on separate 3 × 5″ cards so that you can easily insert new entries in alphabetical order. If you are using a computer, construct your list in a file that is separate from the paper. In each entry include all the information you will need in your bibliography. You may also want to include information you would need (such as the library call number) to find that source again.

Note cards

After you evaluate the source (see section 37) and decide the information may be useful, record the information on note cards (either 3 × 5″ or 4 × 6″ cards), to summarize, paraphrase, or record a quotation (see section 38). Use parentheses or brackets to record your thoughts on how you can use this source in your paper. Limit each note card to one short aspect of a topic so you can reorder the cards later as you organize the whole project.

Label the note card with the author's last name and shortened title, if needed, in the upper right-hand corner. Use a short phrase in the upper left-hand corner as a subject heading. As you write the information, include the exact page numbers and indicate whether the information is a summary, paraphrase, or quotation.

37 Evaluating Sources

We live in an age of information—such vast amounts of information that we cannot know everything about a subject. All of that information that comes streaming at us in newspapers, magazines, the media, books, journals, brochures, Web sites, and so on, is also of very uneven quality. People want to convince us to depend on their data, buy their products, accept their viewpoints, vote for their candidates, agree with their opinions, and rely on them as experts.

We sift and make decisions all the time about which information we will use based on how we evaluate the information. Evaluating sources, then, is a skill we need all the time, and applying that skill to research papers is equally important. Listed here are some stages in the process of evaluating sources for those research papers.

For additional material on evaluating sources on the Internet, see section 41.

Getting started

As you begin searching for information, ask yourself what kinds of information you are looking for and where you are likely to find appropriate sources for that kind of information. You want to be sure that you are headed in the right direction as you launch into your search, and this too is part of the evaluation process—evaluating where you are most likely to get the right kind of information for your purpose.

What kind of information are you looking for?

Do you want facts? Opinions? News reports? Research studies? Analyses? Historical accounts? Personal reflections? Data? Public records? Scholarly essays reflecting on the topic? Reviews?

Where would you find such information?

Which sources are most likely to be useful? Libraries with scholarly journals, books, and government publications? Public libraries with popular magazines? The Internet? Newspapers? Community records? Someone on your campus?

If, for example, you are searching for information on some current event, a reliable newspaper such as the *New York Times* will be a useful source, and it is likely to be available in a university library, a public library, and on the Web. If you need some statistics on the U.S. population, government census documents in libraries and on the Internet will be appropriate places to search. But if you want to do research into local history, the archives of the local government offices and local newspaper are better places to start. Consider whether there are organizations designed to gather and publish the kinds of information you are seeking. And be sure to ask yourself if the organization's goal is to be objective or to gain support for its viewpoint.

Evaluating bibliographic citations

Before you spend time hunting for a source or read it, begin by looking at the following information in the citation to evaluate whether it is worth finding or reading.

1. Author

Credentials

■ How reputable is the person (or organization) listed there?

What is the author's educational background?
What has the author written in the past about this topic?
Why is this person considered an expert or a reliable authority?

You can learn more about the person by checking the Library of Congress to see what else the person has written, and the *Book Review Index* and *Book Review Digest* may lead you to reviews of other books by this person. Your library may have citation indexes in the person's field that will lead you to other articles and short pieces by this person that have been cited by others.

For biographical information you can read *Who's Who in America* or the *Biography Index.* There may also be information about the person in the publication such as listing of previous writings, awards, and notes about the author. Your goal is to get some sense of who this person is and why it is worth reading what that person wrote before you plunge in and begin reading. That may be important as you write the paper and build your case. For example, if you are citing a source to show the spread of AIDS in Africa, which of these sentences strengthens your argument?

"Dr. John Smith notes that the incidence of AIDS in Africa has more than doubled in the last five years."

(or)

"Dr. John Smith, head of the World Health Organization committee studying AIDS in African countries, notes that the incidence of AIDS in Africa has more than doubled in the last five years."

References

Did a teacher or librarian or some other person who is knowledgeable about the topic mention this person?
Did you see the person listed in other sources that you've already determined to be trustworthy?

When someone is an authority, you may find other references to this person. Or this person's viewpoint or perspective may be important to read.

Institution or affiliation

- What organization, institution, or company is the person associated with?
- What are the goals of this group?
- Does it monitor or review what is published under its name?
- Might this group be biased in some way? Are they trying to sell you something or convince you to accept their views? Do they conduct disinterested research?

2. Timeliness

- When was the source published? (For Web sites, look at the "last revised" date at the end of the page.)
- Is that date current enough to be useful, or might there be outdated material?
- Is the source a revision of an earlier edition? If so, it is likely to be more current, and a revision indicates that the source is sufficiently valuable to revise. Check a library catalog or *Books in Print* to see if you have the latest edition.

3. Publisher/producer

- Who published or produced the material?
- Is that publisher reputable? For example, a university press or a governement agency is likely to be a reputalbe source that reviews what it publishes.
- Is the group recognized as an authority?
- Is the publisher or group an appropriate one for this topic?
- Might the publisher be likely to have a particular bias? (For example, a brochure printed by an anti-abortion, right-to-life group is not going to argue for abortion.)
- Is there any review process or fact checking? (If a pharmaceutical company publishes data on a new drug it is developing, is there evidence of outside review of the data?)

4. Audience

- Can you tell who the intended audience is? Is that audience appropriate for your purposes?
- Is the material too specialized or too popular or brief to be useful? (A three-volume study of gene splitting is more than you need for a five-page paper on some

genetically transmitted disease. But a half-page article on a visit to the Antarctica won't tell you much about research into ozone depletion going on there.)

Evaluating content

When you have the source in hand, you can evaluate the content by keeping in mind the following important criteria:

- **Accuracy** Are the facts accurate? Do they agree with other information you've read? Are there sources for the data given?
- **Comprehensiveness** Is the topic covered in adequate depth? Or is it too superficial or limited to only one aspect that, therefore, overemphasizes only one part of the topic?
- **Credibility** Is the source of the material generally considered trustworthy? Does the source have a review process or do fact checking? Is the author an expert? What are the author's credentials for writing about this topic?
- **Fairness** If the author has a particular viewpoint, are differing views presented with some sense of fairness? Or are they presented as irrational or stupid?
- **Objectivity** Is the language objective or emotional? Does the author acknowledge differing viewpoints? Are the various perspectives fairly presented? If you are reading an article in a magazine, do other articles in that source promote a particular viewpoint?
- **Relevance** How closely related is the material to your topic? Is it really relevant or merely related? Is it too general or too specific? Too technical?
- **Timeliness** Is the information current enough to be useful? How necessary is timeliness for your topic?

To help you determine the degree to which the criteria just listed are present in the source, try the following:

- Read the preface. What does the author want to accomplish?
- Browse through the table of contents and the index. Is the topic covered in enough depth to be helpful?
- Is there a list of references that look as if the author has consulted other sources and may lead you to useful related material?
- Are you the intended audience? Consider the tone, style, level of information, and assumptions the author makes about the reader. Are they appropriate to your needs?

■ Is the content of the source fact, opinion, or propaganda? If the material is presented as factual, are the sources of the facts clearly indicated? Do you think there's enough evidence offered? Is the coverage comprehensive? (As you learn more about the topic, you will notice that this gets easier as you become more of an expert.) Is the language emotional or objective?

■ Are there broad, sweeping generalizations that overstate or simplify the matter?

■ Does the author use a mix of primary and secondary sources?

■ To determine accuracy, consider whether the source is outdated. Do some cross-checking. Do you find some of the same information elsewhere?

■ Are there arguments that are one-sided with no acknowledgment of other viewpoints?

38 Using Sources

Integrating sources

As you write your paper, you may be incorporating summaries, paraphrases, and quotations from your sources. It is important to weave these in smoothly, to distinguish for the reader whether you are summarizing, paraphrasing, or quoting, and to signal your reader by using signal words (page 118) to introduce and smoothly blend these sources into your writing.

Summaries

Characteristics of summaries:

■ Are written in your own words
■ Include only the main points, omitting details, facts, examples, illustrations, direct quotations, and other specifics
■ Use fewer words than the source

WRITING A SUMMARY

A summary is a brief statement of the main idea in a source, using your own words. Include a citation to the source.

■ Do not have to be in the same order as the source
■ Are objective and do not include your own interpretation.

Use summaries if the source has unnecessary detail, the writing is not particularly memorable or worth quoting, or you want to keep your writing concise.

2. Paraphrases

Characteristics of paraphrases:

■ Have approximately the same number of words as the source
■ Include all main points and important details in the source
■ Use your own words, not those of the source
■ Keep the same organization as the source
■ Are more detailed than a summary
■ Are objective and do not include your interpretation.

WRITING A PARAPHRASE

A paraphrase restates the information from a source, using your own words. Include a citation to the source.

3. Quotations

Guidelines for using quotations:

■ Use quotations as evidence, support, or further explanation of what you have written. Quotations are not substitutes for stating your point in your own words.
■ Before you include the quotation, indicate what point the quotation is making and why that quotation is relevant.
■ Use quotations sparingly. Too many quotations strung together with very little of your own writing make a paper look like a scrapbook of pasted-together sources, not a thoughtful integration of what is known about a subject.

USING QUOTATIONS

A quotation is the record of the exact words of a written or spoken source and is set off by quotation marks. All quotations should have citation to the source.

■ Use quotations that illustrate an authority's viewpoint or style or that would not be as effective if rewritten in different words.

■ Introduce quotations with signal words (see next page for examples).

For guidelines on punctuation quotations, see section 22.

Using signal words

As you include summaries, paraphrases, and quotations in your papers, you need to integrate them smoothly so that there is no sudden jump or break between the flow of your words and the source material. Use the following strategies to prepare your readers and to create that needed smooth transition into the inserted material.

Use signal phrases

Signal words or phrases let the reader know a quotation will follow. Choose a phrase or word that is appropriate to the quotation and indicates the relationship to the ideas being discussed.

> In 1990 when the United Nations International Human Rights Commission predicted "there will be an outburst of major violations of human rights in Yugoslavia within the next few years" (14), few people in Europe or the United States paid attention to the warning.
>
> (UNITED NATIONS INTERNATIONAL HUMAN RIGHTS COMMISSION. *THE FUTURE OF HUMAN RIGHTS IN EASTERN EUROPE.* NEW YORK: UNITED NATIONS, 1990.)

Explain the connection

Always explain the connection between a quotation you use and the point you are making. Show the logical link, or add a follow-up comment that integrates the quotation into your paragraph.

> **Quotation not integrated into the paragraph**
> Modern farming techniques are different from those used twenty years ago. John Hession, an Iowa soybean grower, says, "Without a computer program to plan my crop allotments or to record my expenses, I'd be back in the dark ages of guessing what to do." New computer software programs are being developed commercially and are selling well.
>
> (HESSION, JOHN. PERSONAL INTERVIEW. 27 JULY 1998.)

SOME COMMON SIGNAL WORDS

according to	considers	observes
acknowledges	denies	points out
admits	describes	predicts
argues	disagrees	proposes
asserts	emphasizes	rejects
comments	explains	reports
complains	finds	responds
concedes	insists	suggests
concludes	maintains	thinks
condemns	notes	warns

The quotation here is abruptly dropped into the paragraph, without an introduction and without a clear indication from the writer how Mr. Hession's statement fits into the ideas being discussed.

Quotation revised

Modern farming techniques differ from those of twenty years ago, *particularly in the use of computer programs for planning and budgeting.* John Hession, an Iowa soybean grower *who relies heavily on computers, confirms this* when he notes, "Without a computer program to plan my crop allotments or to record my expenses, I'd be back in the dark ages of guessing what to do." Commercial software programs *such as those used by Mr. Hession, for crop allotments and budgeting,* are being developed and are selling well.

The added words in italics explain how Mr. Hession's statement confirms the point being made.

PLAGIARISM

Plagiarism results when writers fail to document a source so that the words and ideas of someone else are presented as the writer's own work.

Avoiding plagiarism

What information needs to be documented?

When we use the ideas, findings, data, and conclusions, arguments, and words of others, we need to acknowledge that we are borrowing their work and inserting in our own by documenting. Consciously or unconsciously passing off the work of others as our own results in the form of stealing known as plagiarism, an act that has serious consequences for the writer who plagiarizes.

If you summarize, paraphrase, or use the words of someone else (see pages 116–117), provide documentation for those sources.

CITING SOURCES

In some cultures, educated writers are expected to know and incorporate the thinking of great scholars. It may be considered an insult to the reader to mention the names of the scholars, implying that the reader is not educated enough to recognize the references. However, in American writing this is not the case, and writers are always expected to acknowledge their sources and give public credit to the source.

What information does not need to be documented?

Common knowledge, that body of general ideas we share with our readers, does not have to be documented. Common knowledge consists of the following:

- Standard information on a subject that your readers know
- Information that is widely shared and can be found in numerous sources.

HINT

AVOIDING PLAGIARISM

To avoid plagiarism, read over your paper and ask yourself whether your readers can properly identify which ideas and words are yours and which are from the sources you cite. If that is clear, then you are not plagiarizing.

For example, it is common knowledge among most Americans aware of current energy problems that solar power is one answer to future energy needs. But forecasts about how widely solar power may be used in twenty years or estimates of the cost effectiveness of using solar energy would be the work of some person or group studying the subject, and documentation would be needed.

Field research you conduct also does not need to be documented, although you should indicate you are reporting your own findings.

Original version

Researchers studying human aggression are discovering that, in contrast to the usual stereotypes, patterns of aggression among girls and women under some circumstances may mirror or even exaggerate those seen in boys and men. And while women's weapons are often words, fists may be used too.

> ABIGAIL ZUGER, "A FISTFUL OF HOSTILITY IS FOUND IN WOMEN." *NEW YORK TIMES* 28 JUL. 1998, B9.

Plagiarized version

Women can be as hostile as men. According to Abigail Zuger, researchers studying human aggression are discovering that, in contrast to the usual stereotypes, patterns of aggression among girls and women under some circumstances may mirror or even exaggerate those seen in boys and men. And while women's weapons are often words, fists may be used too (B9).

Revision

An acceptable revision of the plagiarized version would have either a paraphrase or summary in the writer's own words or would indicate, with quotation marks, the exact words of the source. (See page 117.)

VIII

Online

This section deals with using the Internet: what kinds of information are available, how to find information, how to evaluate what you find, and how to cite online sources. You'll also find Web addresses for many useful sites.

continued ▶

39 Research Online

Online searching for information can be very fruitful because it connects you to vast resources in distant places that you can access quickly and easily. But it's important to have a clear sense of which kinds of information are available online and which are better searched for in libraries or other sources such as the community or your campus.

What is available on the Internet?

The Internet is useful when searching for the following kinds of information:

- **Government sources** The federal government has numerous sites on the Internet with large quantities of information produced by various government bureaus and agencies, in addition to information produced by legislative action. You can also check for references to appropriate government publications that your library may have on the shelves.

- **Library catalogs online** You can search many libraries online to find other materials on your topic, materials that your library may not have and may be able to borrow for you. You can also read titles and abstracts to get a sense of what's available on the topic. These online catalogs are especially useful for compiling a working bibliography to start your search. Some of the major libraries online also have searchable databases and lists of resources in various areas that may be useful.

- **Current news** The major American newspapers and magazines have Web sites where you can read about recent events or rapidly changing conditions, and you can search the sites for past information. In most cases, however, these archives only go back a few years.

- **Some older books** Several projects, such as Project Bartleby, the English Server at Carnegie Mellon University, and Project Gutenberg, are dedicated to making available online older books whose copyrights have expired. Other projects are dedicated to making rare or hard-to-find older resources available online.

- **Information relevant to a field of study or major** If you start with the sites listed in Fields of Study in section 40, you'll quickly find the Web sites that have collected links to information about that field.

What is available in the library?

Your library is more useful for the following kinds of information:

- **Major works in the field (books, journals, references)**
  Although some books, reference works, and other
  important resources are being made available on the
  Web, most major studies, histories, references, and so
  on, are in the library, not on the Internet. Some scholarly
  journals are now available on the Web, and some
  electronic journals and magazines too, but they may
  require readers to subscribe or may make only a
  sampling of their contents available on the Web at no
  charge. Most major scholarly books and journals,
  reference works, and magazines are in your library, not
  on the Internet.
- **Historical sources and textbooks** Most older books and
  other materials such as textbooks that are important or
  useful sources of information are in libraries, not on the
  Internet.
- **Databases** Your library is the place to look for those
  databases that charge or require the purchase of a CD-ROM.

Finding information on the Internet

When you begin your search, refine your topic, formulate research questions, and follow other general research strategies as explained in section 36. You will also need to
evaluate your sources because the lack of control or moni-
toring on the Internet means that along with much valuable
information, there is also a great deal of worthless or simply
wrong information available too. See section 41 on evaluating Internet sources. Because the Web is constantly changing, there is also a lot of transient information—information
that is constantly changing. What is available one day when
you surf the Net may be different or gone when you return.

Strategies for searching the Internet

Different types of tools available
- **Search engines** Search engines work by searching among
  the contents of public sites on the Internet for key terms
  that you indicate. The search engine returns a list of sites
  that include the key term. Because various search engines
  work differently, each will turn up different results. Be sure
  to read any help files the search engine site offers so you
  use it effectively. Also, some sites have their own search

engines to help you find information on various parts of
that site.

- **Subject categories or directories** These indexes or
directories organize Web resources by categories such
as "health," "entertainment," and "business." Most
have subdirectories under the main headings. These
lists are particularly useful when you are looking for
suggestions for a topic, for a quick look at the types of
information available on that topic, or for ways to phrase
key terms for searches.
- **Newsgroups and listservs** Newsgroups are open forums
on the Usenet network where anyone can post a message
on the topic of the forum. Listservs are e-mail discussion
groups in which participants have to subscribe to the list.
Any message from any member of the listserv goes to all
the subscribers. The listowner may or may not moderate
what appears by controlling which message gets through
to the list.
- **Web sites with collections of information** Section 40
lists addresses for many Web sites that compile large
quantities of information. For example, under "Fields of
Study" there, you will find sites with many links to
information in the particular field, and the government sites
will be collections of documents relevant to various areas of
the government such as census data, congressional bills
under consideration, world health surveys, and so on.

Different ways to search

Use your detective skills to think about different ways
to start and which leads to follow. When you think cre-
atively, you'll find a variety of kinds of sites, sites beyond
the ordinary or expected ones.

Sample search Suppose your assignment is to research
your major and you want to learn more about job opportunities in that major. Here are some different ways to approach
your search:

- You can go to general job search sites to see what they
have listed.
- Try the resource lists and directories in that academic field
(see section 40) because some of the Web sites list
relevant job opportunities.
- At some university Web sites, the department's page
includes job opportunities.
- Look at U.S. Census report data to see what you can find
there. In other federal government sites, you'll find
government studies of prospects for various fields.

- Try Web sites of large companies in that field to see what they list as job openings. (Some online yellow pages search engines list the Web addresses in addition to the street and city locations.)
- Tune in to listservs and newsgroups of people in that area of work to see what they are discussing.
- Use a few search engines to see what they turn up.

   (There will be some similarities in their listings, but there will also be different ones in each. But be prepared to find that the search engine turns up more items than you want to read.)

Using search engines on the Web

Search engines differ in the way that they search, the documents they search, and the options for searching that they offer. So, before using any search engine, read the "help" file or any explanations offered on the site that will give you a better idea of how to use it effectively.

As you will find out when you read guidelines for various search engines, AltaVista permits you to select the language to search in; HotBot permits you to specify the date, media type, and so on, to search through; and Infoseek permits you to ask questions. DejaNews searches newsgroup postings. The search engines differ in the way that they suggest you include search terms such as "and" or "not."

What are search terms (Boolean terms)?

To narrow your search, you can define the topic and reduce the number of irrelevant findings by using various search terms in combination with the words in your topic. Knowing how to use these search terms will save you time and result in better searches.

AND   AND is the most useful and most important term. It tells the search engine to find your first word AND your second word or term. However, AND can cause problems if you use it with two terms that are likely to appear together in several contexts.

Suppose you'd like some information about the Chicago Bulls, the basketball team. If you type in "Chicago AND Bulls," you will get many references to Chicago and to bulls. Because Chicago is the center of a large meatpacking industry, many of the references returned by the search engine will be about the meatpacking industry in Chicago.

OR   OR is not always a helpful term because you may find too many combinations with OR.

If you type in "American OR economy," you will get thousands of references to documents containing the word "American" or the word "economy."

Use OR when a key term may appear in two different ways.

If you want information on sudden infant death syndrome, try "sudden infant death syndrome OR SIDS."

NEAR   NEAR is a term that appears only on some search engines, and it can be very useful. It tells the search engine to find documents with both words but only when they appear near each other, usually within a few words.

If you were looking for information on mobile homes, you'd have a problem because almost every site has a "click here to return to the home page." The search engine would find thousands of those sites that also have the word "mobile" in them. Using NEAR would help solve that problem.

NOT   NOT tells the search engine to find a reference that contains one term but not the other.

If you want information about the life of Martin Luther King, Jr., but not his assassination (because that would be too much to cover in your paper), you would type "Martin Luther King, Jr. NOT assassination."

40 Web Resources

INDEX TO WEB RESOURCES

1. **Writing**
   Here you find links to style manuals; grammar and writing handouts; MLA, APA, and *Chicago Manual* sites; dictionaries; a thesaurus; *Bartlett's Familiar Quotations;* and information on business, social science, and technical writing.
   Use these sites for help with writing.

2. General Subjects

This is a particularly useful collection of links to huge subject directories; online books, journals, and newspapers; scholarly societies and electronic discussion groups; colleges; and search engines.
Use these sites for initial searches across a broad area and for links to articles and books available online.

3. Fields of Study

Here you'll find links to sites that focus on specific fields of study such as education, history, science, or engineering.
Use these sites for more specialized information in a particular field of study.

4. Government

Vast sites link to all the government agencies and have online publications of data collected by all branches of the government, from health to population to Web sites for governments of other countries.
Use these sites for data, statistics, or studies you think might have been done by government agencies and for information about all branches of government and the work they do.

5. Libraries Online

These are links to online libraries. Many have search engines, databases that are available to all users, and collections of useful links.
Use these links to find out what else has been written about your topic and what books and journals can be loaned to your library if your library does not have those materials. Use the Uncover keyword search to find articles on your topic (abstracts of the articles are free).

1. Writing

■ Writer's Resources: Inkspot: <http://www.inkspot.com>
■ Writing Guides
   Strunk and White, *Elements of Style:* <http://www.columbia.edu/acis/bartleby/strunk>
   Writing Lab OWLs (Online Writing Labs):
   National Writing Centers Association OWLs:<http://departments.colgate.edu/diw/NWCAOWLS.html>

Purdue University:<http://owl.english.purdue.edu>
University of Missouri: <http://www.missouri.edu/
~writery/writehelp.html>

■ Writing in Special Fields
Business Writing: <http://www.inkspot.com/genres/biz
.html>
<http://owl.english.purdue.edu/bw>
Journalism: <http://www.inkspot.com/genres/
journalism.html>
Social Science Writing:
<http://www.pol.adfa.oz.au/essay
.intro.html>
Technical and Scientific Writing: <http://www.inkspot
.com/genres/tech.html>

■ References
Bartlett's Familiar Quotations: <http//www.columbia.edu/
acis/bartleby/bartlett>
Biographical Dictionary: <http://s9.com/biography>
Merriam Webster Dictionary: <http://www.m-w.com/
dictionary>
Online Dictionaries: <http://www.bucknell.edu/~rbeard/
diction.html>
Roget's Thesaurus: <http://humanities.uchicago.edu/
forms_unrest/ROGET.html>

2. General Subjects

■ Search Engines
Alta Vista: <http://www.altavista.digital.com>
Deja News: <http://wwwdejanews.com>
Einet Galaxy: <http://www.einet.net>
Excite: <http://www.excite.com>
HotBot: <http://www.hotbot.com/>
Infoseek: <http://www.infoseek.com>
Lycos: <http://www.lycos.com>
Northern Lights: <http://www.nlsearch.com/>
Starting Point: <http://www.stpt.com>
Webcrawler: <http://www.webcrawler.com>
Yahoo: <http://www.yahoo.com>

■ General Subject Directories
Argus Clearinghouse for Subject-Oriented Internet
Resource Guides: <http://www.clearinghouse.net>
Awesome List: <http://www.clark.net/pub/journalism/
awesome.html>
Internet Public Library: <http://www.ipl.org>

WWW Virtual Library: <http://vlib.stanford.edu/Overview.html>

■ Books Online

Electronic Texts and Publishing Resources: <http://lcweb.loc.gov/global/etext/etext.html>

The On-Line Book Page: <http://www.cs.cmu.edu/Web/books.htm>

The On-Line Book Page by Author: <http://www.cs.cmu.edu:8001/Web/bookauthors.html>

Project Bartleby: <http://www.cc.columbia.edu/acis/bartleby>

Project Gutenberg: <http://promo.net/pg>

■ Electronic Listservs and Newsgroups
<http://tile.net/lists/>

Usenet: <http://www.cis.ohio-state.edu/hypertext/faq/bngusenet/news/groups/top.html>

■ Journals and Periodicals Online
<http://english.hss.cmu.edu/Journals.html>

■ Newspapers, News Services, and Magazines Online

Chronicle of Higher Education: <http://chronicle.com>

EcolaNewsstand: <http://www.ecola.com>

Electronic Newsstand: <http://enews.com/>

Electronic Journals: <http://www.library.ubc.ca/ejour/>

Pathfinder (Time Warner publications): <http://pathfinder.com>

New York Times: <http://nytimes.com>

Reuters News Media: <http://www.reuters.com>

USA Today: <http://usatoday.com>

Wall Street Journal: <http://www.wsj.com>

WWW Virtual Library Electronic Journals: <http://www.edoc.com/ejournals>

■ Scholarly Electronic Conferences

Directory of Scholarly and Professional E-Conferences: <http://www.n2h2.com/KOVACS>

■ Scholarly Societies

Alliance for Computers and Writing: <http://english.ttu.edu/acw/>

American Astronomical Society: <http://www.aas.org>

American Institute of Physics: <http://www.aip.org>

American Philosophical Society: <http://www.udel.edu/APA/>

Association of Teachers of Technical Writing: <http://english.ttu.edu/ATTW/>

Council of Biology Editors: <http://www.cbe.org/cbe/>

Home Pages of Scholarly Societies Project: <http://www
.lib.uwaterloo.ca/society/overview.html>

National Academy of Sciences: <http://www.nas.edu>

National Council of Teachers of English: <http://www.
ncte.org/>

Web Pages of Scholarly Societies Project: <http://www
.lib.uwaterloo.ca/society/webpages.html>

■ Universities in the United States
http: <///www.clas.ufl.edu/CLAS/american-universities.html>

3. Fields of Study

An excellent place to start is the Academic Information Index. It has a rich collection of links for most major academic
fields of study: <http://www.academicinfo.net/table.html>

■ Business
CommerceNet: <http://www.commerce.net>

Internet Business Library: <http://www.bschool.ukans.
edu/intbuslib/virtual.htm>

Nijenrode: <http://www.nijenrode.nl/nbr/index.html>

Open Market: <http://www.openmarket.com>

■ Education
AskEric: <http://ericir.syr.edu>

Educational Technology: <http://www.educause.edu/>

EdWeb: <http://k12.cnidr.org:90>

ERIC: <http://www.aspensys.com/eric/index.html>

■ Humanities
American Studies:
<http://www.georgetown.edu/crossroads/asw>

Arts: <http://wwar.world-arts-resources.com>

Communication: <http://alnilam.ucs.indiana.edu:1027/
sources/comm.html>

Cultural Studies: <http//humanitas.ucsb.edu/shuttle/
cultural.html>

English:
Academic Info English and ESL/EFL: <http://www.
academicinfo.net/englang.html>

American Literature: <http://www.academicinfo.net/
amlit.html>

Carnegie Mellon English Server: <http://english-server
.hss.cmu.edu>

English Literature: <http://www.academicinfo.net/
englit.html>

Literary Resources on the Net: <http://dept.english.
upenn.edu/~jlynch/Lit>

Foreign Language and Literature:

Academic Info Foreign Lang Study: <http://www.academicinfo.net/lang.html>

Foreign Language Resources on the WWW: <http://www.itp.berkeley.edu/~thorne/HumanResources.html>

History:

Academic Info History:<http://www.academicinfo.net/hist.html>

ED U2-History: <http://www.wco.com/~ejia/EDU/history.htm>

Gateway to World History: <http://www.hartford-hwp.com/gateway/index.html>

Horus' Web Links to History Resources: <http://www.ucr.edu/h-gig/horuslinks.html>

Humanities: Voice of the Shuttle: <http://humanitas.ucsb.edu>

Philosophy:

<http://www.academicinfo.net/phil.html>

HIPPIAS Philosophy Search Engine: <http://hippias.evansville.edu>

Philosophy in Cyberspace: <http://www-personal.monash.edu.au/~dey/phil/>

Political Science:

Academic Info Pol Sci: <http://www.academicinfo.net/polisci.html>

<http://www.lib.umich.edu/libhome/Documents.center/polisci.html>

Political Sci Research Resources: <http://php.indiana.edu/~rmtucker/polssrc.html>

Psychology:

Clinical Psychology Resources: <http://www.psychologie.unibonn.de/kap/links_20.htm>

CyberPsychLink: <http://cctr.umkc.edu/user/dmartin/psych2.html>

Psych Web: <http://www.psych-web.com>

Religion: Academic Info Religion Main Index: <http://www.academicinfo.net/religindex.html>

Social Science Information Gateway: <http://sosig.ac.uk/welcome.html>

Sociology:

Academic Info Sociology: <http://www.academicinfo.net/soc.html>

Socioweb: <http://www.socioweb.com/~markbl/socio-web>

Sociology Internet Resources: <http://www.wcsu.ctstateu.edu/sociolsci/socres.html>

Women's Studies:

    Academic Info Women's Studies: <http://www.
      academicinfo.net/women.html>

    <http://sunsite.unc.edu/cheryb/women>

    Women's Studies (R)E-Sources on the Web:<http://
      scriptorium.lib.duke.edu/women/cyber.html>

■ Natural Sciences

Chemistry:

    Chemdex: <http://www.shef.ac.uk/~chem/chemdex/>

    Chemistry Web Home Page: <http://www.ssc.ntu.edu.
      sg: 8000/chemweb/htmlj/>

Computer Science:

    Computer Technology-Engineering and Technology:
    <http://galaxy.einet.net/galaxy/Engineering-and-
      Technology/Computer-Technology.html>

    EE/CS Mother Site: <http://wwwee.stanfordedu/soe/
      ieee/eesites.html>

Environmental Studies:

    Best Environmental Resources Directory: <http://www.
      ulb.ac.be/ceese/meta/cds.html>

    Directory of Environmental Resources on the Internet:
      <http://envirosw.com>

    EnviroInfo: <http://www.deb.uminho.pt/fontes/
      enviroinfo/>

Mathematics:

    Mathematics Information Servers: <http://www.
      math.psu.edu/MathLists/Contents.html>

    MathSearch: <http://www.maths.usyd.edu.au:8000/
      MathSearch.html>

Medicine:

    Medscape: <http://www.medscape.com>

    Medweb: <http://www.emory.edu/WHSCL/medweb
      .html>

Physics:

    Academic Info Physics: <http://www.academicinfo.net/
      physics.html>

    Physics around the World: <http://www.tp.umu.se/
      TIPTOP/paw/>

Science: Discovery Channel Online: <http://www.discovery
    .com>

4. Government

■ Bureau of the Census: <http://www.census.gov>

■ CIA: <http://www.odci.gov>

■ Fedworld: <http://www.fedworld.gov>

- National Institutes of Health: <http://www.nih.gov>
- Nonprofit: <http://www.nonprofit.gov>
- Statistics: <http://www.stat-usa.gov/stat-usa.html>
- Thomas: <http://thomas.loc.gov>
- U.S. and foreign governments: <http://www.eff.org/govt.html>
- White House: <http://www.whitehouse.gov>
- World Health Organization: <http://www.who.ch>

5. Libraries online

- American Library Association: <http://www.ala.org>
- Internet Public Library: <http://www.ipl.org>
- Law Library: <http://www.io.org/~jgcom/librlaw.htm>
- LIBCAT (guide to library resources on the Internet): <http://www.metronet.lib.mn.us/lc/lcl.html>
- Library of Congress: <http://lcweb.loc.gov>
- Libweb: <http://sunsite.berkeley.edu/Libweb>
- Uncover (a keyword index to thousands of periodicals; abstracts are free, articles available by interlibrary loan or for a fee): <http://uncweb.carl.org/uncover/unchome.html> (Carlweb: <http://www.carl.org/carlweb/>)
- Uncoverweb: <http://wncweb.carl.org>

 Evaluating Internet Sources

Evaluating Internet sources is particularly difficult because anyone can put up anything on the Internet. There is no way to monitor or to check facts, although there are some site ratings you can check. For a discussion of companies that review Internet sites, see <http://www.tiac.net/users/hope/findqual.html>. At the end of that essay by Hope Tillman, you will find a discussion of various ratings.

Some criteria to consider as you read Internet sources:

1. Authorship

Is there an author or organization clearly indicated?
  If so, review the questions about authorship listed in section 37. Can the author be contacted? If an e-mail address is given, you can use the "finger" command to learn the person's name.
What can you find out about the author?
  If there is no information on the site, use a search engine or search Usenet. You may find the author's

home page or other documents that mention this
person. Or look up the person on the Internet
Directory of Published Writers (<http://www.writers.
net>). If the person is associated with a university,
look at the university Web site.

If there is an organization sponsoring the page, what
can you learn about the organization and who they are?
You can search the site by following links to the home
page or going back a previous level on the site by
deleting the last part of the address, after the various
"/" marks. Another way to find the organization is to
go to the View menu at the top of your Web browser
and open the Document Information window where
the owner of the document is listed.

Does the organization take responsibility for what's
on the site? Does it monitor or review what's there?
Look at the address. If it ends in ".edu," it's an
educational institution. If it ends in ".gov," whatever
you find should be fairly objective government-
sponsored material. Addresses with ".org" are usually
nonprofit organizations that are advocacy groups. For
example, the Sierra Club, at http://www.sierra.org, is
an advocacy group whose postings conform to their
goals of environmental protection. Information posted
by advocacy groups may be accurate but not entirely
objective. If the site has a ".com" address, it's most
likely promoting or selling something.

2. Accuracy of information

Is there documentation to indicate the source of the
information? There may be a link to the original
source of the information.
Can you tell how well researched the information is?
Are criteria for including information offered?
Is there a bibliography or links to other useful sites?
Has the author considered information on those sites
or considered viewpoints represented there?
Is the information current? When was it updated?
(Check at the bottom of the page for a "last revised"
date. If there are numerous dead links, that's a clue
the page has not been updated recently.)
Is there an indication of bias on the site?
Does the site have any credentials, such as being rated
by a reputable rating group? If you see a high rating,
is that because of the reliability of the content or the

quality of the graphics? (An attractive page is not a reason for accepting its information as reliable.)

3. Goals of the site

What is the purpose of the site? To advertise? To persuade? To provide information? To provide disinformation?

For example, some groups intent on helping their candidate get elected put up sites that emphasize the opponent's weaknesses or ridicule the opponent. Some sites are owned by hate groups that manage to disguise their real purpose.

Are the goals of the site clearly indicated?

Who is the intended audience?

Is there a lot of flash and color and gimmicks to attract attention? Is that masking a lack of sound information or a blatant attempt to get you to buy or do something?

4. Access

How did you find the site?

Were there links from reputable sites?

From ads?

If you found the site through a search engine, that means only that the site has the keywords in your topic prominently placed or used with great frequency.

If you found the site by browsing through a subject directory, it may mean only that someone at that site registered it with that directory.

Internet Resources on Evaluation

Some Web sites that have useful essays on evaluating sources and links to other useful sites are the following:

- Alexander, Jan, and Marsha Tate. "Teaching Critical Evaluation Skills for the World Wide Web": <http://www.science.widener.edu/~withers/webeval.htm>
- Grassian, Esther. "Thinking Critically about World Wide Web Resources": <http://www.library.ucla.edu/libraries/college/instruct/critical.htm>
- Harris, Robert. "Evaluating Internet Research Sources": <http://www.sccu.edu/faculty/R_Harris/evalu8it.htm>
- Jacobson, Trudi, and Laura Cohen. "Evaluating Internet Sites": <http://www.albany.edu/library/internet/evaluate.html>
- Kirk, Elizabeth. "Evaluating Information Found on the Internet":

<http://milton.mse.jhu.edu:8001/research/education/
net.html>
- Ormondroyd, J., Engle, M., & Cosgrave, T. "How to critically analyze information sources": http://www.library.cornell.edu/okuref/research/skill26.htm
- Patterson, Shawn, Alan Wendt, and Robert Schroeder. "Evaluating and Citing Internet Resources": <http://www.udmercy.edu/htmls/Academics/library/webpage>
- Richmond, Betsy. "Ten C's for Evaluating Internet Resources": <http://www.uwec.edu/Admin/Library/10cs.html>
- Smith, Alastair. "Evaluation of Information Sources": <http://www.vuw.ac.nz/~agsmith/evaln/evaln.htm>
- Stegall, Nancy. "Online Writing Support Center: Using Cybersources": <http://www.devryphx.edu/lrnresrc/dowsc/integrty.htm>
- Tillman, Hope. "Evaluating Quality on the Net": <http://www.tiac.net/users/hope/findqual.html>

42 Citing Internet Sources

MLA online citation

The Internet and Online Databases

Starting on page 162, section 43 describes formats for CD-ROMs and other portable databases. These are available commercially and in libraries. But when you are citing information from the Internet or from online databases, you are using databases that are not bought in stores or carried around. Although access to the Internet is free, services such as AOL or online databases such as Nexis charge a fee. Thus, some additional elements to be included in the citation are the publication medium (that is, Online), the name of the computer service or computer network through which the database is accessed, and the date of access.

Material accessed through a computer service or network such as the World Wide Web
There are two groups of such materials:

1. **Materials with a print source** These materials were or are still available in print. Include information on both the print and online versions, including the date when the online version was accessed.

Meharry, William. "Beta-Carotene May Be
        Dangerous to Your Health." <u>New York Times</u>
        24 January 1996, late ed.: B3. New York
        Times Online. Online. Lexis-Nexis. 15
        August 1996.

2. Materials with no print source   These materials do
not indicate a print source. Include as much information
as is available.

Sapir, Mortimer. "Dangers of Anesthesia."
        <u>American Medical Encyclopedia</u>. Online.
        Prodigy. 9 Aug. 1995.

Citing sources from the World Wide Web

The MLA has posted the only guidelines they authorize
on their Web site: <http://www.mla.org/set_stl.htm>
Include as many items from the following list as you can.

1. **Name**   Include the name of the author, editor,
   compiler, or translator, in reversed order, followed by
   an abbreviation such as "ed." or "trans."
2. **Title**   Title of the work (poem, short story, article,
   and so on) within a scholarly project, database, or
   periodical, in quotation marks; or title of a posting
   (found in the subject line) to a discussion list or
   forum, in quotation marks, followed by the
   description "Online posting"
3. **Title of book (underlined)**
4. **Name of editor, compiler, and so on.**   If not already
   cited as the first entry (see number 1), include the
   name of the editor, compiler, or translator of the text,
   preceded by an abbreviation such as "Ed." or
   "Trans."
5. **Publication information for any print version of the
   source**
6. **Title of project or site**   Title of the scholarly
   project, database, periodical, or professional or
   personal site (underlined); or, for a professional or
   personal site with no title, a description such as
   "Home page"
7. **Name of editor**   If available, the name of the editor
   of the scholarly project or database
8. **Version number of the source**   If not listed as part
   of the title, include the version number of the source
   or, for a journal, the volume number, issue number, or
   other identifying number

9. **Date**   The date of electronic publication, of the latest update, or of the posting
10. **List or forum name**   For a posting to a discussion list or forum, the name of the list or forum
11. **Numbers**   The total number of pages, paragraphs, or other sections, if numbered.
12. **Organization or institution name**   The name of the sponsoring organization or institution
13. **Date of access**   Date you accessed the source
14. **Electronic address**   The electronic address or URL, in angle brackets: < >

Scholarly project

Smith, Terry Donovan, and Katie Johnson, "Domestic Life in 19th Century English Drama." The 19th Century London Stage: An Exploration. University of Washington School of Drama 4 Feb. 1998 last update 1/3/97 Jack Wolcott and Joan Robertson, eds. <http://artsci.washington.edu/ drama-phd/19title.html>

Professional site

Women's Studies Program. Chun-Hui Sophie Ho, Ed. Purdue U. June 1997 5 Feb. 1998 <http://www.sla.purdue.edu/academic/idis/ womens-studies/main.html>

Personal site

Kaplan, Hannah. Home page. 9 Feb. 1998 <http://www.mcs.com/~dkaplan/hannah.html>

Book

Yonge, Charlotte. Henrietta's Wish; or, Domineering: a Tale. 2nd ed. London, 1853. Ed. Perry Willett. 4 Feb. 1998. Indiana U. 9 Feb. 1998 <http://www.indiana.edu/~letrs/ vwwp/yonge/henrietta.html>

Poem

Eliot, T. S. "Whispers of Immortality." Poems. New York, 1920. Project Bartleby Archive. Columbia U. 1994. 6 Feb. 1998 <http://www. columbia.edu/acis/bartleby/eliot/22.html>

Article in a reference database

"Kennedy, John Fitzgerald." Encyclopedia.com.
        1998. Electric Library. 5 Feb. 1998 <www.
        encyclopedia.com/articles/06898.html>

Article in a journal

Materassi, Mario. "The Forest and the Trees:
        Some Notes on the Study of Multiculturalism
        in Italy." American Quarterly 48.1 (1996):
        110-120. 6 Feb. 1998 <http://direct.press.
        jhu.edu/journals/american_quarterly/v048/48.
        1materassi.html>

Article in a magazine

Surowiecki, James. "The Taming of the
        Barbarians." Slate 5 Feb. 1998. 6 Feb.1998
        <http://www.slate.com/motleyfool/98-02-05/
        motleyfool.asp>

Posting to a discussion list

Maxon, Don. "Blending ESL and Bilingual
        Education." Online posting. 5 Jan. 1998.
        Dave Sperling Presents ESL Discussion
        Center Forum for Teachers: Bilingual
        Education. 6 Feb. 1998 <http://www.eslcafe.
        com/discussion/ds/index.cgi?read=2>

APA online citation

Electronic Sources

In addition to the guidelines in the most recent *Publication Manual of the American Psychological Association* (4th edition), guidelines are posted on their Web site (<http://www.apa.org/journals/webref.html>) on how to cite information from the Internet and the World Wide Web. The goal of references remains the same—to credit the author and to help your reader find the material. Cite electronic correspondence (e-mail, electronic discussion groups, and so on) as personal communication in your text but do not include it in your reference list.

All references begin with the same information (or as much as possible) that is included for a print source. Place World Wide Web information at the end of the reference. Use "Retrieved from" and the date of retrieval because the content of documents can be changed or revised and can be removed from the site. For databases and CD-ROM materials not online, see section 44. For formats for in-text citations of electronic sources in APA format, see section 44.

Internet and the World Wide Web

Examples here are from the World Wide Web, and a similar format can be used to cite gopher or ftp sources with the medium and path adequately identified.

1. Journal

Klein, D. F. (1997). Control groups in pharmacotherapy and psychotherapy evaluations. Treatment, 1. Retrieved February 9, 1998 from the World Wide Web: http://journals.apa.org/treatment/vol1/ 97_a1.html.

2. Newspaper Article

Freiberg, P. (1998, February). We know how to stop the spread of AIDS: So why can't we? Psychologists point to a need for more work in the policy arena. APA Monitor [Newspaper, selected stories on line.] Retrieved February 9, 1998 from the World Wide Web: http://www.apa. org/monitor/ aids.html.

3. Abstract

McCutchen, A., Francis, M., & Kerr, S. (1997). Revising for meaning: Effects of knowledge and strategy [Abstract]. Journal of Educational Psychology 89, 667–676. Retrieved February 9, 1998 from the World Wide Web: http://www.apa.org/journals/edu/ 1297ab.thml#8.

4. Online Abstract

Brindelstein, C., & Chen, S. (1993). The social interaction of small children in task differentiated groups. [Online]. Childhood Socializing, 14, 234–241. Abstract from: DIALOG File: PyscINFO Item: 46-12144.

5. Online Journal, Subscriber Based

Cross-Cultural Speech Interference Study Group. (1995, October 21). Signaling

affirmation in informal conversation:
Contrasting behaviors of Hispanics and African-
Americans [720 paragraphs]. Online Journal of
Contrastive Cultural Behaviors [On-line serial].
Available: Doc. No. 99.

Other formats for citing online sources

Chicago Manual Style

For information on citing electronic sources in *Chicago Manual* style, see section 45.

Council of Biology Editors (CBE)

For information on citing electronic sources in CBE style, see section 45.

Additional resources

When writers started using online sources for writing, various groups began to offer their citation formats. If you are seeking information about other online citation formats, these resources will help:

■ Janice Walker's home page: <http://www.columbia.edu/cu/cup/cgos/idx_basic.html>
Janice Walker, whose format is endorsed by the Alliance for Computers and Writing (ACW), suggests the following basic components of a citation for both MLA and APA:

MLA
Author's Lastname, Author's Firstname. "Title of Document." Title of Complete Work (if applicable). Version or File Number, if applicable. Document date or date of last revision (if different from access date). Protocol and address, access path or directories (date of access).

■ Web site

Crouse, Maurice. "Citing Electronic
Information in History Papers." 26 Mar.
1998. <http://www.people.memphis.edu/
~mcrouse/elcite.html> (14 Aug. 1998).

■ E-mail, Listserv, and Newsgroups:

Gillespie, Paula. "Re: Ethical Query." (7 Apr.
1998). <wcenter@ttacs6.ttu.edu> (14 Aug.
1998).

Thelen, Liz. "Color printer." Personal e-mail
    (9 Aug. 1998).

APA

Author's Last Name, Initial (s). (Date of Work, if known). Title of work. *Title of complete work.* [protocol and address] [path] (date of message or visit).

■ Web site

Crouse, M. (1998). Citing electronic
information in history papers. http://www.
people.memphis.edu/~mcrouse/elcite.html (14
Aug. 1998).

■ E-mail, Listserv, and Newsgroups

Gillespie, P. (7 Apr. 1998). "Re:
Ethical Query." *wcenter@ttacs6.ttu.edu.*
Available: http://www.ttu.edu/lists/wcenter/
9804/0070.html (14 Aug. 1998).

Personal e-mail is not listed in the References list when using APA style. See page 142.

■ CIC Electronic Journals Collections: <http://ejournals. cic.net>
The CIC (Committee on Institutional Cooperation, a group of major midwestern universities) sponsors this site, which lists and connects to electronic journals in the fields of Arts and Humanities, Business and Economy, Computers and Internet, Education, Entertainment, Environmental Science and Nature, Government, Health, History, Literature and Poetry, Mathematics, Meteorology, Reference, Regional, Science, Social Science, and Society and Culture. Some of the journals listed under these categories offer electronic citation information in the guidelines for submission of essays. Or you can read the online issues to see how bibliographies in recent articles are formatted.

■ IFLA (International Federation of Library Associations and Institutions): <http://www.ifla.org/I/training/ citation/citing.htm>
This site lists style guides and resources on the Internet, books, software, and e-mail notes about electronic citation.

■ Internet Public Library Citing Electronic Resources: <http://www.ipl.org/ref/QUE/FARQ/netciteFARQ.html>
This site lists books and other sites on the Web (including the Yahoo Category: Internet Citation) that offer information on electronic citation.

■ Li, Xia and Nancy B. Crane. *Electronic Styles: A Handbook for Citing Electronic Information.* 2nd ed. Medford, N. J. : Information Today Inc., 1996.

■ National Library of Canada. "Citing Electronic Sources: A Bibliography": <http://www.nlc.bnc.ca/services/eciting.html> This site lists other Internet sites, articles, and theses with information on citing electronic sources. It also includes an annotated bibliography on style guides in print format, separated into (1) publications focusing entirely on citing electronic information, and (2) publications on citing sources, including sections devoted to citing electronic publications.

IX

Documentation

This section contains information on documenting your sources in the paper, in endnotes or footnotes, and in the list of works cited (or reference list) at the end of the paper. The formats for MLA, APA, *The Chicago Manual of Style,* and Council of Biology Editors (CBE) are explained and illustrated. Indexes to the examples for the notes and bibliographies will lead you to the ones you need, and there is also a list of style manuals for fields that use other documentation formats.

YOUR **QUESTION**   SECTION

continued ▶

When you research a topic, you are building on the work of others, and your work, in turn, contributes to the pool of knowledge about the topic for others who will read and depend on your research. Thus, it is necessary to give credit to those whose work you use and to document your sources so completely that readers of your work can find the sources you used.

Documentation formats vary, depending on the field of study. Organizations such as newspapers and other publishing companies, businesses, and large organizations often have their own formats that are explained in their style manuals.

For English and other humanities, use the format of the Modern Language Association (MLA):

Gibaldi, Joseph. *MLA Handbook for Writers of Research Papers*. 5th ed. New York: MLA, 1999.

Some of the major features of MLA style are as follows:

- For in-text citations, give the author's last name and page number of the source, preferably within the sentence rather than after it.
- Use full first and last names and middle initials of authors.
- Capitalize all major words in titles, and underline titles or put them in italics. Enclose article titles in quotation marks.
- In "Works Cited" list at the end of the paper, give full publication information, alphabetized by author.

THREE ASPECTS OF MLA FORMAT TO CONSIDER

1. **In-text citations**
   In your paper you need parenthetical references to your sources to acknowledge wherever you use the words, ideas, and facts you've taken from your sources.

2. **Endnotes**
   If you need to add material that would disrupt your paper if it were included in the text, include such notes at the end of the paper.

3. **Works Cited list**
   At the end of your paper, include a list of the sources from which you have quoted, summarized, or paraphrased.

In-text citations

The purpose of in-text citations is to help your reader find the appropriate reference in the list of works cited at the end of the paper. Current MLA format recommends parenthetical references (not footnotes), depending on how much information you include in your sentence or in your introduction to a quotation. Try to be brief, but not at the expense of clarity, and remember to use signal words and phrases (see section 38).

INDEX TO EXAMPLES OF MLA IN-TEXT CITATIONS

1. Author's name not given in the text

If the author's name is not in your sentence, put the last name in parentheses, leave a space with no punctuation, and then put the page number.

> Recent research on sleep and dreaming
> indicates that dreams move backward in time
> as the night progresses (Dement 72).

2. Author's name given in the text

If you include the author's name in the sentence, only the page number is needed in parentheses.

> Freud states that "a dream is the
> fulfillment of a wish" (154).

3. Two or more works by the same author

If you used two or more different sources by the same author, put a comma after the author's last name and include a shortened version of the title and the page reference. If the author's name is in the text, include only the title and page reference.

> One current theory emphasizes the principle that dreams express "profound aspects of personality" (Foulkes, Sleep 144).

> Foulkes's investigation shows that young children's dreams are "rather simple and unemotional" ("Children's Dreams" 90).

4. Two or three authors

If your source has two or three authors, either name them in your sentence or include the names in parentheses.

> Jeffrey and Milanovitch argue that the recently reported statistics for teenage pregnancies are inaccurate (112).

(or)

> The recently reported statistics for teenage pregnancies are said to be inaccurate (Jeffrey and Milanovitch 112).

5. More than three authors

If your source has more than three authors, either use the first author's last name followed by "et al." (which means "and others") or list all the last names.

> The conclusions drawn from a survey on the growth of the Internet, conducted by Martin et al., are that global usage will double within two years (36).

(or)

> Recent figures on the growth of the Internet indicate that global usage will double within two years (Martin, Ober, Mancuso, and Blum 36).

6. Unknown author

If the author is unknown, use a shortened form of the title in your citation.

More detailed nutritional information in food
labels is proving to be a great advantage to
diabetics ("New Labeling Laws" 3).

7. Corporate author or government document

Use the name of the corporation or government agency,
shortened or in full. It is better to include long names in your
sentence to avoid extending the parenthetical reference.

The United Nations Regional Flood
Containment Commission has been studying
weather patterns that contribute to flooding
in Africa (4).

8. An entire work

For an entire work, it is preferable to include the author's
name in the text.

Lafmun was the first to argue that small
infants respond to music.

9. A work in an anthology

Cite the name of the author of the work, not the editor of the
anthology, in the sentence or in parentheses.

When Millet refers to her childhood, she uses
vague references such as "in my younger days"
(14) rather than specific ages or dates.

10. A literary work

For classic prose works, such as novels or plays available in
several editions, provide more information than a page reference to the edition you used. A chapter number, for example, might help readers locate the reference in any copy.
Give the page number first, add a semicolon, and then give
other identifying information.

In The Prince, Machiavelli reminds us that
while some manage to jump from humble
origins to great power, such people find
their greatest challenge to be staying in
power: "Those who rise from private
citizens to be princes merely by fortune
have little trouble in rising but very
much trouble in maintaining their position"
(23; Ch.7).

For verse plays and poems, omit page numbers and cite by division (act, scene, canto, etc.) and line, with periods separating the various numbers. For lines, initially use the word "line" or "lines" and then afterward, give the numbers alone.

> Eliot again reminds us of society's
> superficiality in "The Lovesong of J. Alfred
> Prufrock": "There will be time, there will
> be time/To prepare a face to meet the faces
> that you meet" (lines 26-27).

11. A multivolume work

When you cite a volume number as well as a page reference for a multivolume work, separate the two by a colon and a space. Do not use the words "volume" or "page."

> In his History of the Civil War, Jimmersen
> traces the economic influences that
> contributed to the decisions of several
> states to stay in the Union (3: 798-823).

12. Indirect source

If you have to rely on a secondhand source in which some-one's quoted words appear in a source written by someone else, start the citation with the abbreviation "qtd. in."

> Although Newman has established a high
> degree of accuracy for such tests, he
> reminds us that "no test like this is ever
> completely and totally accurate" (qtd. in
> Mazor 33).

13. Two or more sources

If you cite more than one work in your parenthetical reference, separate the references by a semicolon.

> Recent attempts to control the rapid
> destruction of the rain forests in Central
> America have met with little success
> (Costanza 22; Kinderman 94).

Endnotes

When you have additional comments or information that would disrupt the paper, cite the information in endnotes numbered consecutively through the paper. Put the number after the punctuation at the end of the phrase, clause, or sentence containing the material you are referring to. Use a superscript (raised) number above the line, with no punctuation. Leave no extra space before the number and one extra space after if the reference is in the middle of the sentence and two extra spaces when the reference number is at the end of the sentence.

> The treasure hunt for sixteenth-century pirate loot buried in Nova Scotia began in 1927,[3] but hunting was discontinued when the treasure seekers found the site flooded at high tide.[4]

At the end of your paper, begin a new sheet with the heading "Notes," but do not underline or put the heading in quotation marks. Leave a one-inch margin at the top, center the heading, double-space, and then begin listing your notes. For each note, indent five spaces, use a superscript number (the number raised above the line), number, and begin the note. Double-space, and if the note continues on the next line, begin that line at the left margin. The format is slightly different from that used in the Works Cited section: the author's name appears in normal order, followed by a comma, the title, publisher, date in parentheses, and a page reference.

> [3]Some historians argue that this widely accepted date is inaccurate. See Jerome Flynn, <u>Buried Treasures</u> (New York: Newport, 1978): 29–43.

> [4]Avery Jones and Jessica Lund, "The Nova Scotia Mystery Treasure," <u>Contemporary History</u> 9 (1985): 81–83.

If you are asked to use footnotes instead of endnotes, place them at the bottoms of pages, beginning four lines (two double spaces) below the text. Single-space footnotes, but double-space between them. Number them consecutively through the paper.

Works Cited list

The Works Cited is a list of all the sources cited in your paper, not other materials you read but didn't refer to. Arrange the list alphabetically by the last name of the author, and if there is no author, alphabetize by the first word of the title (but not the articles *a, and,* or *the*).

For the Works Cited section, begin a new sheet of paper, leave a one-inch margin at the top, center the heading "Works Cited" (with no underline or quotation marks), and then double-space before the first entry. For each entry, begin at the left margin for the first line and indent five spaces (or one-half inch) for additional lines in the entry. Double-space throughout. Place the Works Cited list at the end of your paper after the notes, if you have any.

There are three parts to each reference: (1) author, (2) title, and (3) publishing information. Each part is followed by a period and two spaces.

INDEX TO EXAMPLES OF MLA WORKS CITED

Books
1. One author
2. Two or three authors
3. More than three authors
4. More than one work by the same author
5. A work that names an editor
6. A work with an author and an editor
7. A work that names a translator
8. A work by a corporate author
9. A work by an unknown author
10. A work that has more than one volume
11. A work in an anthology
12. Two or more works in the same anthology
13. An article in a reference book
14. Introduction, foreword, preface, or afterword
15. A work with a title within a title
16. Second or later edition
17. Modern reprint
18. A work in a series
19. A work with a publisher's imprint
20. Government publication
21. Proceedings of a conference

Articles in Periodicals
22. Scholarly journal with continuous paging
23. Scholarly journal that pages each issue separately
24. Monthly or bimonthly magazine article
25. Weekly or biweekly magazine article
26. Newspaper article

27. Unsigned article
28. Editorial or letter to the editor
29. Review of a work
30. Article in microform collection of articles

Electronic Sources

CD-ROMs and Other Portable Databases
31. Material accessed from a periodically published database on CD-ROM
32. Publication on CD-ROM
33. Publication on diskette
34. Work in more than one published medium

The Internet and Online Databases
35. Material accessed through a computer service or network such as the World Wide Web

Other Sources
36. Computer software
37. Television or radio program
38. Record, tape cassette, or CD
39. Film or video recording
40. Live performance of a play
41. Musical composition
42. Work of art
43. Letter, memo, e-mail communication, or public online posting
44. Personal interview
45. Published interview
46. Radio or television interview
47. Map or chart
48. Cartoon
49. Advertisement
50. Lecture, speech, or an address
51. Pamphlet
52. Published dissertation
53. Abstract of a dissertation
54. Unpublished dissertation

Books

| Author(s). | Book Title. | Place of publication: Publisher, |

| year of publication. |

↗ year of publication.

(indent 5 spaces)

Articles in Periodicals

| Author(s). | "Title of the Article." Journal Title | volume |

number,   date of publication: page numbers.

(indent 5 spaces)

Books

1. One author

Joos, Martin. The Five Clocks. New York:
    Harcourt, Brace, and World, 1962.

2. Two or three authors

Mellerman, Sidney, John Scarcini, and Leslie
    Karlin. Human Development: An Introduction
    to Cognitive Growth. New York: Harper, 1981.

3. More than three authors

Either name only the first and add "et al." ("and others") or
give all names in the order they appear on the title page.

Spiller, Robert, et al. Literary History of
    the United States. New York: Macmillan,
    1960.

(or)

Spiller, Robert, Harlan Minton, Michael Upta,
    and Gretchen Kielstra. Literary History
    of the United States. New York:
    Macmillan, 1960.

4. More than one work by the same author

Use the author's name in the first entry only. From then on,
type three hyphens and a period and then begin the next title. Alphabetize by title.

Newman, Edwin. A Civil Tongue. Indianapolis:
    Bobbs-Merrill, 1966.

---.Strictly Speaking. New York: Warner Books,
    1974.

5. A work that names an editor

Use the abbreviation "ed." for one editor (for "edited by")
and "eds." for more than one editor.

Kinkead, Joyce A., and Jeanette Harris, eds.
     Writing Centers in Context: Twelve Case
     Studies. Urbana: NCTE, 1993.

6. A work with an author and an editor

Give the editor's name after the title. Before the name put
the abbreviation "Ed." (for "Edited by") or "Eds." for more
than one editor.

Frankfurter, Felix. The Diaries of Felix
     Frankfurter. Ed. Thomas Sayres. Boston:
     Norton, 1975.

7. A work that names a translator

Use the abbreviation "Trans." (for "Translated by").

Sastre, Alfonso. Sad Are the Eyes of William
     Tell. Trans. Leonard Pronko. Ed. George
     Wellwarth. New York: New York UP, 1970.

8. A work by a corporate author

United States Capitol Society. We, the People:
     The Story of the United States Capitol.
     Washington, National Geographic Soc.,
     1964.

9. A work by an unknown author

Report of the Commission on Tests. New York:
     College Entrance Examination Board, 1970.

10. A work that has more than one volume

For two or more volumes of a work cited in your paper, put
references to volume and page numbers in the parenthetical references. If you are citing only one of the volumes
in your paper, state the number of that volume in the
Works Cited and give publication information for that volume alone.

Rutherford, Ernest. The Collected Papers.
     3 vols. Philadelphia: Allen and Unwin,
     1962-65.

Stowe, Harriet Beecher. "Sojourner Truth, the
     Libyan Sibyl." 1863. The Heath Anthology
     of American Literature. Ed. Paul Lauter

et al. 2nd ed. Vol. 1. Lexington: Heath,
1994. 2425–33.

11. A work in an anthology

State the author and title of the work first, then the title and
other information about the anthology, including page numbers on which the selection appears.

Dymvok, George E., Jr. "Vengeance." Poetry in
the Modern Age. E. Jason Metier. San
Francisco: New Horizons. 1994. 54.

Licouktis, Michelle. "From Slavery to
Freedom." New South Quarterly 29 (1962):
87–98. Rpt. in Voices of the Sixties:
Selected Essays. Ed. Myrabelle McConn.
Atlanta: Horizons, 1995. 12–19.

12. Two or more works in the same anthology

Include a complete entry for the collection and then cross-
reference the works to that collection. In the cross-reference
include the author and title of the work, the last name of the
editor of the collection, and the inclusive page numbers.

Batu, Marda, and Hillary Matthews, eds. Voices
of American Women. New York: Littlefield,
1995.

Jamba, Shawleen. "My Mother's Not Going Home."
Batu and Matthews 423–41.

13. An article in a reference book

If the article is signed, give the author first. If it is unsigned, give the title first. If articles are arranged alphabetically, omit volume and page numbers. When citing
familiar reference books, list only the edition and year of
publication.

"Bioluminescence." The Concise Columbia
Encyclopedia. 1983 ed.

14. Introduction, foreword, preface, or afterword

Start the entry with the author of the introductory part.

Bruner, Jerome. Introduction. Thought and
Language. By Lev Vygotsky. Cambridge:
M.I.T., 1962. v–xiii.

15. A work with a title within a title

If a title normally underlined appears within another title, do not underline it or put it inside of quotation marks.

Lillo, Alphonso. <u>Re-Reading Shakespeare's Hamlet from the Outside</u>. Boston: Martinson, 1995.

16. Second or later edition

Ornstein, Robert E. <u>The Psychology of Consciousness</u>. 2nd ed. New York: Harcourt, 1977.

17. Modern reprint

After the title of the book, state the original publication date. In the publication information that follows, put the date of publication for the reprint.

Weston, Jessie L. <u>From Ritual to Romance</u>. 1920. Garden City: Anchor-Doubleday, 1957.

18. A work in a series

If the title page or preceding page of the book indicates it is part of a series, include the series name, without underlines or quotation marks, and the series number, followed by a period, before the publication information.

Waldheim, Isaac. <u>Revisiting the Bill of Rights</u>. Studies of Amer. Constitutional Hist. 18. New York: Waterman, 1991.

19. A work with a publisher's imprint

For books under imprints or special names that usually appear with the publisher's name on the title page, include the imprint name and then a hyphen and the name of the publisher.

Tamataru, Ishiko. <u>Sunlight and Strength</u>. New York: Anchor-Doubleday, 1992.

20. Government publication

United States. Office of Education. <u>Tutor-Trainer's Resource Handbook</u>. Washington: GPO, 1973.

21. Proceedings of a conference

Treat the published proceedings of a conference like a book and include information about the conference if such information is not included in the title.

Esquino, Luis. <u>Second Language Acquisition in the Classroom</u>. Proc. of the Soc. for Second Language Acquisition Conference, Nov. 1994, U of Texas. Dallas: Midlands, 1995.

Articles in periodicals

22. Scholarly journal with continuous paging

Most scholarly journals have continuous pagination throughout the whole volume for the year. To find a particular issue on the shelf, you need only the volume number and the page, not the issue number.

Delbruch, Max. "Mind from Matter." <u>American Scholar</u> 47 (1978) : 339-53.

23. Scholarly journal that pages each issue separately

If each issue of the journal starts with page 1, then include the issue number.

Barthla, Frederick, and Joseph Murphy. "Alcoholism in Fiction." <u>Kansas Quarterly</u> 17.2 (1981): 77-80.

24. Monthly or bimonthly magazine article

Lillio, Debra. "New Cures for Migraine Headaches." <u>Health Digest</u> Oct. 1995: 14-18.

25. Weekly or biweekly magazine article

For a magazine published every week or every two weeks, give the complete date beginning with the day and abbreviating the month. Do not give the volume and issue numbers.

Isaacson, Walter. "Will the Cold War Fade Away? " <u>Time</u> 27 Feb. 1987: 40-45.

26. Newspaper article

Provide the author's name and the title of the article, then the name of the newspaper as it appears on the masthead, omitting any introductory article such as "The." If the city of publication is not included in the name, add the city in square brackets but not underlined, after the name: Journal-Courier [Trenton]. If the paper is nationally published, such as Wall Street Journal, do not add the city of publication.

Strout, Richard L. "Another Bicentennial." New
    York Times 10 Nov. 1994, late ed.: A9+.

27. Unsigned article

"Trading Lives." Newsweek 21 Apr. 1993:
    87-89.

28. Editorial or letter to the editor

If you are citing an editorial, add the work "Editorial," without an underline or in quotation marks, after the title of the editorial.

"Watching Hillary's Defense Team at Play."
    Editorial. Washington Times 5 Jan. 1996,
    late ed.: A18.

29. Review of a work

Include the reviewer's name and title of the review, if any, followed by the words "Rev. of" (for "Review of"), the title of the work being reviewed, a comma, the word "by," and then the author's name. If the work has no title and is not signed, begin the entry with "Rev. of" and in your Works Cited; alphabetize under the title of the work being reviewed.

Kauffmann, Stanley. "Cast of Character." Rev.
    of Nixon, dir. Oliver Stone. New Republic
    22 Jan. 1996: 26-27.

Rev. of The Beak of the Finch, by Jonathan
    Weiner. Science Weekly 12 Dec. 1995: 36.

30. Article in microform collection of articles

Gilman, Elias. "New Programs for School
    Reform." Charleston Herald 18 Jan. 1991:
    14. Newsbank: School Reform 14 (1991) :
    fiche 1, grids A7-12.

Electronic sources
CD-ROMs and other portable databases

Sources in electronic form that are stored on CD-ROMs, diskettes, and magnetic tapes and have to be read on computers are portable databases. State the medium of publication (such as CD-ROM or diskette), the vendor's name, and the date of electronic publication.

31. Material accessed from a periodically published database on CD-ROM

If no printed source is indicated, include author, title of material (in quotation marks), date of material (if given), title of database (underlined), publication medium, name of vendor, electronic publication date.

```
Anstor, Marylee. "Nutrition for Pregnant
     Women." New York Times 12 Apr. 1994, late
     ed.: C1. New York Times Ondisc. CD-ROM.
     UMI-Proquest. Oct. 1994.
```

32. Publication on CD-ROM

For CD-ROM publications without updates or regular revisions, cite like books, and add the medium of publication.

```
Mattmer, Tobias. "Discovering Jane Austen."
     Discovering Authors. Vers. 1.0. CD-ROM.
     Detroit: Gale, 1992.
```

33. Publication on diskette

Diskette publications are cited like books with an added description of the medium of publication.

```
Lehmo, Jarred. Ethnicity in Dance. Diskette.
     Chicago: U of Chicago P, 1995.
```

34. Work in more than one published medium

Some electronic publications appear as packages of materials in different publication media. For example, a CD-ROM may be packaged with a diskette. Cite such publication packages as you would a CD-ROM product, specifying the media in the package.

```
History of Stage Costuming in Europe. CD-ROM,
     videodisc. Philadelphia: Michelson, 1995.
```

The internet and online databases

Online databases are not bought in stores or carried around. Although access to the Internet is free, services such as AOL or databases such as Lexis-Nexis charge a fee. Some additional elements to be included in the citation are

the publication medium (that is, Online), the name of the
computer service or computer network through which the
database is accessed, and the date of access.

35. Material accessed through a computer service or network such as the World Wide Web

For a more complete discussion of MLA format for online
sources, see section 42, pages 139–142. There you'll find explanations of how to cite materials with a print source as
well as materials with no print source, plus descriptions of
each of the items to be listed in a citation. These items are
also explained in the guidelines posted by the MLA on their
Web site and are the only guidelines the MLA authorizes:

http://www.mla.org/set_stl.htm

The items to list for an online source include as many of
the following as you can:

- **Name** of author, editor, compiler, or translator, in
  reversed order, followed by an abbreviation, if needed,
  such as "ed." or "trans."
- **Title of the work** (or subject line of a posting) in quotation
  marks, followed by the description "Online posting"
- **Title of book** (underlined)
- **Name of editor, compiler, etc.** if not already included as
  the first entry, preceded by an abbreviation such as
  "Ed."or "Trans."
- **Publication information** for any print version of the source
- **Title of project or site,** underlined. For a professional or
  personal site with no title, a description such as "Home page"
- **Name of editor,** if available
- **Version number of the source** or, for a journal, volume
  number, issue number, or other identifying number
- **Date** of electronic publication, of the latest update, or of
  the posting
- **List or forum name**
- **Numbers** (total) of pages, paragraphs, or other sections, if
  numbered
- **Organization or institution name**
- **Date of access** (when you accessed the source)
- **Electronic address or URL** in angle brackets: < >

Professional site

Women's Studies Program. Chun-Hui Sophie Ho,
    Ed. Purdue U. June 1997 5 Feb. 1998
    <http://www.sla.purdue.edu/academic/idis/
    womens-studies/main.html>

Personal site

Kaplan, Hannah. Home page. 9 Feb. 1998
     <http://www.mcs.com/~dkaplan/hannah.html>

Article in a journal

Materassi, Mario. "The Forest and the Trees:
     Some Notes on the Study of Multiculturalism
     in Italy." American Quarterly 48.1 (1996):
     110–120. 6 Feb. 1998 <http://direct.press.
     jhu.edu/journals/american_quarterly/v048/48
     .1materassi.html>

Article in a magazine

Surowiecki, James. "The Taming of the
     Barbarians." Slate 5 Feb. 1998. 6
     Feb.1998 <http://www.slate.com/motleyfool/
     98-02-05/motleyfool.asp>

Posting to a discussion list

Maxon, Don. "Blending ESL and Bilingual
     Education." Online posting. 5 Jan. 1998.
     Dave Sperling Presents ESL Discussion
     Center Forum for Teachers: Bilingual
     Education. 6 Feb. 1998 <http://www.eslcafe.
     com/discussion/ds/index.cgi?read=2>

For examples of other types of online citations, see section 42.

Other sources

36. Computer software

Citations are similar to citations for CD-ROM or diskette materials

McProof. Vers. 3.2.1. Diskette. Salt Lake
     City: Lexpertise, 1987.

37. Television or radio program

Include the episode title (in quotation marks), program title (underlined), series title (no underline or quotation marks), name of the network, call letters and city of the local station, broadcast date. If pertinent, add information such as names of performers, director, or narrator.

"Tall Tales from the West." <u>American Folklore</u>.
     Narr. Hugh McKenna. Writ. Carl
     Tannenberg. PBS. WFYI, Indianapolis. 14
     Mar. 1995.

38. Record, tape cassette, or CD

Depending on which is emphasized, cite the composer, con-
ductor, or performer first. Then list the title (underlined),
artist, medium—if not a compact disc (no underline or quotation marks), manufacturer, year of issue (if unknown, include
"n.d." for "no date"). Place a comma between manufacturer
and date, with periods following all other items.

Perlman, Itzhak. <u>Mozart Violin Concertos Nos.</u>
     <u>3 & 5</u>. Weiner Philarmoniker Orch. Cond.
     James Levine. Deutsche Grammophon, 1983.

Schiff, Heinrich. <u>Five Cello Concertos</u>. By
     Antonio Vivaldi. Academy of St. Martin-
     in-the-Fields. Dir. Iona Brown.
     Audiocassette. Philips, 1984.

39. Film or video recording

Begin film citations with the title (underlined), include the
director, distributor, and the year, and perhaps the names
of the writer, performers, and producer. Treat a videocassette, videodisc, slide program, or filmstrip like a film, and
give the original release date and the medium before the
name of the distributor.

<u>Richard III</u>. By William Shakespeare. Dir. Ian
     McKellen and Richard Loncrain. Perf. Ian
     McKellen, Annette Bening, Jim Broadbent,
     and Robert Downey, Jr. MGM/UA, 1995.

Renoir, Jean, dir. <u>The Rules of the Game</u> [Le
     Règle du Jeu]. Perf. Marcel Dalio and
     Nora Gregor. 1937. Videocassette. Video
     Images, 1981.

40. Live performance of a play

Include the theater and city where the performance was
given, separated by a comma and followed by a period, and
the date of the performance.

<u>Inherit the Wind</u>. By Jerome Lawrence and
     Robert E. Lee. Dir. John Tillinger. Perf.

George C. Scott and Charles Durning.
Royale Theatre, New York. 23 January 1996.

41. Musical composition

If the composition is known only by number, form, or key, do
not underline or use quotation marks. If the score is published, cite it like a book and capitalize abbreviations such as
"no." and "op."

Bach, Johann Sebastian. Brandenburg
     Concertos.

Bach, Johann Sebastian. Orchestral Suite
     No. 1 in C Major.

42. Work of art

Monet, Claude. Rouen Cathedral. Metropolitan
     Museum of Art, New York. Masterpieces of
     Fifty Centuries. New York: Dutton, 1970. 316.

43. Letter, memo, e-mail communication, or public online posting

Blumen, Lado. Letter to Lui Han. 14 Oct. 1990.
     Lado Blumen Papers. Minneapolis Museum of
     Art Lib., Minneapolis.

Milan, Theresa. "Greetings." E-mail to Simon
     Mahr. 18 Sept. 1995.

44. Personal interview

Kochem, Prof. Alexander. Personal interview.
     18 Apr. 1995.

45. Published interview

Goran, Nadya. "A Poet's Reflections on the End
     of the Cold War." By Leonid Tuzman.
     International Literary Times 18 Nov.
     1995: 41-44.

46. Radio or television interview

Netanyahu, Benyamin. Interview with Ted
     Koppel. Nightline. ABC. WABC, New York.
     18 Aug. 1995.

47. Map or chart

Treat a map or chart like a book without an author (see number 9), but add the descriptive label (Map or Chart).

New York. Map. Chicago: Rand, 1995.

48. Cartoon

Adams, Scott. "Dilbert." Cartoon. Journal and
     Courier [Lafayette] 20 Jan. 1996: B7.

49. Advertisement

Apple Computer. Advertisement. GQ, Dec. 1994:
     145-46.

50. Lecture, speech, or an address

Lihandro, Alexandra. "Writing to Learn." Conf.
     on Coll. Composition and Communication
     Convention. Palmer House, Chicago. 23
     Mar. 1990.

Trapun, Millicent. Address. Loeb Theater.
     Indianapolis. 16 Mar. 1995.

51. Pamphlet

Thirty Foods for Your Health. New York:
     Consumers Health Soc., 1996.

52. Published dissertation

If the work was published by University Microfilms International (UMI), add the order number as supplementary information.

Blalock, Mary Jo. Consumer Awareness of Food
     Additives in Products Offered as Organic.
     Diss. U Plainfield, 1994. Ann Arbor: UMI,
     1995. 10325891.

53. Abstract of a dissertation

Begin with the publication information for the original work, and then add the information for the journal that includes the abstract.

McGuy, Timothy. "Campaign Rhetoric of
     Conservatives in the 1994 Congressional

Elections." Diss. Johns Hopkins U, 1995.
<u>DAI</u> 56 (1996): 1402A.

54. Unpublished dissertation

Tibbur, Matthew. "Computer-Mediated
    Intervention in Early Childhood
    Stuttering." Diss. Stanford U, 1991.

Sample pages from an MLA-style research paper

Included here are the following:

1. a sample title page
2. a first page for a paper that does not have a title page
3. a first page for the Works Cited list

Research papers that follow MLA style generally do not
need a title page, but if you are asked to include one, follow
the format shown here.

Proportions shown in margins of sample papers are not
actual but are adjusted to fit space limitations of this book.
Follow actual dimensions shown in margins and your instructor's directions.

1. Sample title page using MLA style

(center title one-third down the page)

A Miracle Drug to Keep Us Young
or Another False Hope?

Michael G. Mitun   *(name)*

Professor Jomale   *(instructor)*
English 102, Section 59   *(course)*
18 November 1999   *(date)*

 1"

2. Sample first page using MLA style

1″   *1/2″*

Mitun

Michael G. Mitun
Professor Jomale
English 102   } *(double-space)*
18 November 1995

            A Miracle Drug to Keep Us Young   } *(double-space)*
                or Another False Hope?   } *(double-space)*

    Even before Ponce de Leon landed in Florida in
1513, searching for a fountain of youth, people
looked for ways to resist the aging process. Among
the unsuccessful cures that we find in history
records are ice baths, gold elixirs, and holding
one's breath. But now modern medicine is opening the
door to new therapies that might work, pills based on
hormones that our bodies produce when we're young but
that decrease as we grow old. At the moment, the most
promising of these hormones is DHEA, the subject of
magazine articles and a television newsmagazine
program ("Natures"; *Eye to Eye*). As medical evidence
continues to appear, the number of believers is
increasing. But most physicians are unwilling to
prescribe DHEA for their patients, and the U.S. Food
and Drug Administration has not approved its sale in
the United States. At the present time, DHEA shows
promise but is not yet the miraculous "fountain of
youth" people have been waiting for.

    At a recent conference hosted by the New York
Academy of Sciences, titled "Dehydroepiandrosterone
(DHEA) and Aging," medical researchers reported on
their studies of DHEA. Burkhard Bilger, one of the
people attending that conference, heard vivid
testimonials about this compound which he describes
as "the most plentiful steroid hormone in the human
body—and the most poorly understood" (26). The
promise of DHEA suggests that we take a closer look
at the evidence to see if medicine really can offer
us a new fountain of youth, though the chief of
biology Dr. Anna McCormick at the National Institute
on Aging warns that there are potential harmful
effects (Jaroff).

1″

3. Sample works cited page using MLA format

 1"   1/2"

Mitun 14

Works Cited

Ames, Donna Spahn. "The Effects of Chronic
    Endurance Training on DHEA and DHEA-S Levels
    in Middle-Aged Men." Diss. U. of New
    Hampshire, 1991.

Bilger, Burkhard. "Forever Young." The Sciences
    Sept./Oct. 1998: 26-30.

Eye to Eye. CBS. WCBS, New York. 15 June 1995.

Fahey, Thomas D. "DHEA." Joe Weider's Muscle and
    Fitness Aug. 1995: 94-97.

Garcia, Homer. "Effects of Dehydroepiandrosterone
    (DHEA) on Brain Tissue." DHEA Transformations
    in Target Tissue. Ed. Milan Zucheffa. London:
    Binn, 1994: 36-45.

---. "Estrogens in Target Tissues." Endocrinology
    136 (1997): 3247-56.

Jaroff, Leon. "New Age Therapy." Time 23 Jan.
    1996: 52.

Health and Aging. Prod. Hormone Therapy Project,
    Middleton Medical School. Videodisc.
    Middleton, 1997.

Li, Min Zhen, ed. The Biologic Role of
    Dehydroepiandrosterone (DHEA). Berlin: de
    Gruyter, 1990.

Mindell, Earl L. "Stay Healthy." Let's Live
    Sept. 1994: 8-14.

"Nature's Other Time-Stopper." Newsweek 7 Aug.
    1995: 49.

Oppenheim, Edgar. "DHEA Offers Promise." Springfield
    Courier 22 June 1995, late ed.: B1. Current
    News Ondisc. CD-ROM. New York: Qube, 1995.

Rabin, Prof. Jonathan. Personal interview. 21
    Oct. 1998.

Rosch, Paul J. "DHEA, Electrical Stimulation,
    and the Fountain of Youth." Stress Medicine
    11.4 (1995): 211-27.

Whaum, Ken. "Re: DHEA testimonials." Online
    posting. 23 Oct. 1998. Newsgroupalt.health.
    aging.natural. 2 Nov. 1998. <http://www.dhea.com/
    discussion/dheabenefits.html>

1"

 **APA Style**

American Psychological Association (APA) format is used to document papers in the behavioral and social sciences. If you are asked to use APA format, consult *The Publication Manual of the American Psychological Association,* (4th ed.). (1994). Washington, DC: American Psychological Association.

APA/MLA similarities
- Both have parenthetical references in the paper to refer readers to the list at the end of the paper.
- Both have numbered notes to include information that would disrupt the writing if included there.
- Both have a reference list of works cited at the end of the paper.
- For both, references include only the sources used in the research and preparation of the paper.

APA/MLA differences
- In APA, the date of publication is included in parenthetical references in the paper and appears after the author's name in the reference list.
- In APA, authors' first and middle names are indicated by initials only.
- In APA, capitalization and use of quotation marks and underlining are different. (See box on page 174.)
- In APA each citation in the References begins with an indent. In MLA, each Works Cited citation begins at the left margin and then indents the following lines.

In-text citations

Include the author's name and date of publication. For direct quotations, include the page number also.

1. Direct quotations

When you quote a source, end with quotation marks and give the author, year, and page number in parentheses.

> Many others agree with the assessment that "this is a seriously flawed study" (Methasa, 1994, p. 22) and do not include its data in their own work.

IMPORTANT FEATURES OF APA STYLE

- In-text citations, give the author's last name and publication year of the source.

- In quotations, put signal words (see page 119) in past tense (such as "Smith reported") or present perfect tense (such as "as Smith has reported").

- Use full last names and initials of first and middle names of authors.

- Capitalize only the first word and proper names in book and article titles, but capitalize all major words in journal titles. Underline titles of books and journals; do not put article titles in quotation marks.

- In References at the end of the paper, give full publication information, alphabetized by author.

EXAMPLES OF APA IN-TEXT CITATIONS

1. Direct quotations
2. Author's name given in the text
3. Author's name not given in the text
4. Work by multiple authors
5. Group as author
6. Work with unknown author
7. Authors with the same last name
8. Two or more works in same parentheses
9. Classical works
10. Specific parts of a source
11. Personal communications
12. World Wide Web

2. Author's name given in the text

Cite only the year of publication in parentheses. If the year also appears in the sentence, do not add parenthetical information. If you refer to the same study again in the paragraph, with the source's name, you do not have to cite the year again if it is clear that the same study is being referred to.

> When Millard (1970) compared reaction times among the participants, he noticed an increase in errors.

> In 1994 Pradha found improvement in short-term memory with accompanying practice.

3. Author's name not given in the text

Cite the name and year, separated by a comma.

> In a recent study of reaction times (Millard, 1970), no change was noticed.

4. Work by multiple authors

For two authors, cite both names every time you refer to the source. Use "and" in the text, but an ampersand (&) in parenthetical material, tables, captions, and the reference list.

> When Glick and Metah (1991) reported on their findings, they were unaware of a similar study (Grimm & Tolman, 1991) with contradictory data.

For three, four, or five authors, include all authors (and date) the first time you cite the source. For additional references, include only the first author's name and "et al." (for "and others"), with no underline or italics.

> Ellison, Mayer, Brunerd, and Keif (1987) studied supervisors who were given no training. Later, when Ellison et al. (1987) continued to study these same supervisors, they added a one-week training program.

For six or more authors, cite only the first author and "et al." and the year for all references.

> Mokach et al. (1989) noted no improvement in norms for participant scores.

5. Group as author

The name of the group that serves as the author (for example, a government agency or a corporation) is usually spelled out every time it appears in a citation. If the name is long but easily identified by its abbreviation and you want to switch to the abbreviation, give the abbreviation in parentheses when the entire name first appears.

In 1992 when the National Institute of Mental Health (NIMH) prepared its report, no field data on this epidemic were available. However, NIMH agreed that future reports would correct this.

6. Work with unknown author

When a work has no author, cite the first few words of the reference list entry and the year.

One newspaper article ("When South Americans," 1987) indicated the rapid growth of this phenomenon.

7. Authors with the same last name

If two or more authors in your reference list have the same last name, include their initials in all text citations.

Until T. A. Wilman (1994) studied the initial survey (M. R. Wilman, 1993), no reports were issued.

8. Two or more works in the same parentheses

When two or more works are cited within the same parentheses, arrange them in the order they appear in the reference list, and separate them with semicolons.

Several studies (Canin, 1989; Duniere, 1987; Pferman & Chu, 1991) reported similar behavior patterns in such cases.

9. Classical works

Reference entries are not necessary for major classical works such as ancient Greek and Roman works and the Bible, but identify the version you used in the first citation in your text. If appropriate, in each citation, include the part (book, chapter, lines).

This was known (Aristotle, trans. 1931) to be prevalent among young men with these symptoms.

10. Specific parts of a source

To cite a specific part of a source, include the page, chapter, figure, or table, and use the abbreviation "p." (for "page") and "chap." (for "chapter").

> No work was done on interaction of long-term memory and computer programming (Sitwa & Shiu, 1993, p. 224), but recently (Takamuru, 1996, chap. 6) reported studies have considered this interaction.

11. Personal communications

Personal communications include letters, memos, some electronic communications (e.g., e-mail, discussion groups, messages on electronic bulletin boards), telephone conversations, and other similar communications. Because the data cannot be recovered, these are included only in the text and not in the reference list. Include the initials and last name of the communicator and as exact a date as possible. (For electronic sources that can be documented, see section 46.)

> According to I. M. Boza (personal communication, June 18, 1995), no population studies of the problem were done before 1993.

12. World Wide Web

To cite a Web site in the text (but not a specific document), include the Web address. No reference entry is needed in the References.

> The Web site for the American Psychological Association (http://www.apa.org) has listed an update on how to cite information found on the World Wide Web.

Footnotes

Content footnotes add important information that cannot be integrated into the text, but they are distracting and should be used only if they strengthen the discussion. Copyright permission footnotes acknowledge the source of quotations that are copyrighted. Number the footnotes consecutively with superscript arabic numerals and include the footnotes on a separate page after the reference list.

References list

Arrange entries in alphabetical order by the author's last name, and for several works by one author, arrange by year of publication with the earliest one first. For authors' names, give all surnames first and then the initials. Use commas to separate a list of two or more names, and use an & (ampersand) before the last name in the list. Capitalize only the first word of the title and the subtitle (and any proper names) of a book or article, but capitalize the name of the journal. Underline (or italicize) book titles, names of journals, and the volume number of the journal.

Start the reference list on a new page, with "References" centered at the top of the page and double-space all entries. Indent the first line of each entry five to seven spaces, the same as a paragraph in the text.

Books

1. One author

> Rico, G. L. (1983). <u>Writing the natural way</u>. Los Angeles: J. P. Tarcher.

2. Two or more works by the same author

Include the author's name in all references and arrange by year of publication, the earliest first.

> Kilmonto, R. J. (1983). <u>Culture and ethnicity</u>. Washington, DC: American Psychiatric Press.

> Kilmonto, R. J. (1989). Comparisons of cultural adaptations. <u>Modern Cultural Studies, 27</u>, 237–243.

3. Two or more authors

> Strunk, W., Jr., & White, E. B. (1979). <u>The elements of style</u> (3rd ed.). New York: Macmillan.

4. Group or corporate author

If the publication is a brochure, list this in brackets.

> Mental Health Technical Training Support Center. (1994). <u>Guidelines for mental health nonprofit agency staffs</u> (2nd ed.) [Brochure]. Manhattan, KS: Author.

EXAMPLES OF APA REFERENCES

Books

1. One author
2. Two or more works by the same author
3. Two or more authors
4. Group or corporate author
5. Unknown author
6. Edited volume
7. Translation
8. Article or chapter in an edited book
9. Article in a reference book
10. Revised edition
11. Multivolume work
12. Technical and research report
13. Report from a university

Articles in Periodicals

14. Article in a journal paged continuously
15. Article in a journal paged separately by issue
16. Article in a magazine
17. Article in a newspaper
18. Unsigned article
19. Monograph
20. Review of a book, film, or video

Electronic Sources

21. Internet and the World Wide Web
22. Online abstract
23. Online journal, subscriber-based
24. Electronic database
25. CD-ROM
26. Computer program or software

Other Sources

27. Information service
28. Dissertation abstract
29. Government document
30. Conference proceedings
31. Interview
32. Film, videotape, performance, or artwork
33. Recording
34. Cassette recording
35. Television broadcast, series, and single episode from a series
36. Unpublished paper presented at a meeting

5. Unknown author

Americana collegiate dictionary (4th ed.). (1995). Indianapolis, IN: Huntsfield.

6. Edited volume

Maher, B. A., & Hueng, N. O. (Eds.). (1964–1972). Progress in experimental personality research (6 vols.). New York: Academic Press.

7. Translation

Lefranc, J. R. (1976). A treatise on probability (R. W. Mateau & D. Trilling, Trans.). New York: Macmillan. (Original work published 1952)

8. Article or chapter in an edited book

Include page numbers of article or chapter.

Riesen, A. H. (1991). Sensory deprivation. In E. Stellar & J. M. Sprague (Eds.), Progress in physiological psychology (pp. 24–54). New York: Academic Press.

9. Article in a reference book

Terusami, H. T. (1993). Relativity. In The new handbook of science (Vol. 12, pp. 247–249). Chicago: Modern Science Encyclopedia.

10. Revised edition

Telphafi, J. (1989). Diagnostic techniques (rev. ed.). Newbury Park, CA: Pine.

11. Multivolume work

Donovan, W. (Ed.). (1979–1986). Social sciences: A history (Vols. 1–5). New York: Hollins.

12. Technical and research report

Birney, A. F., & Hall, M. M. (1981). Early identification of children with written language disabilities (Report No. 81–502). Washington, DC: National Education Association.

13. Report from a university

Lundersen, P. S., McIver, R. L., &
Yepperman, B. B. (1993). Sexual harassment
policies and the law (Tech. Rep. No. 9).
Springfield: University of Central Indiana,
Faculty Affairs Research Center.

Articles in periodicals

14. Article in a journal paged continuously

Schaubroeck, J., Sime, W. E., & Mayes,
B. T. (1991). The nomological validity of the
type A personality. Journal of Applied
Psychology, 76, 143-168.

15. Article in a journal paged separately by issue

Timmo, L. A., & Kikovio, R. (1994). Young
children's attempts at deception. Research in
Early Childhood Learning, 53(2), 49-67.

16. Article in a magazine

Simmons, H. (1995, November 29). Changing
our buying habits. American Consumer, 21,
29-36.

17. Article in a newspaper

Leftlow, B. S. (1993, December 18).
Corporate takeovers confuse stock market
predictions. Wall Street Journal, pp. A1, A14.

18. Unsigned article

New study promises age-defying pills.
(1995, July 27). The Washington Post, p. B21.

19. Monograph

Rotter, P. B., & Stolz, G. (1966).
Generalized expectancies of early childhood
speech patterns. Monographs of the Childhood
Education Society, 36 (2, Serial No. 181).

20. Review of a book, film, or video

If the review is untitled, use the material in brackets as the
title and indicate if the review is of a book, film, or video; the

brackets indicate the material is a description of form and content, not a title.

>   Carmody, T. P. (1982). A new look at medicine from the social perspective [Review of the book Social contexts of health, illness, and patient care]. Contemporary Psychology, 27, 208-209.

Electronic sources

In addition to the guidelines in the most recent Publication Manual of the American Psychological Association (4th ed.), guidelines are posted on their Web site (http://www.apa.org/journals/webref.html) on how to cite information from the Internet and the World Wide Web. The goal of references remains the same—to credit the author and to help your reader find the material. Electronic correspondence (e-mail, electronic discussion groups, and so on) is cited as personal communication in your text but does not need to be included in your reference list.

All references begin with the same information (or as much as possible) that is included for a print source. World Wide Web information is placed at the end of the reference. Use "Retrieved from" and the date of retrieval because the content of documents can be changed or revised and can be removed from the site.

21. Internet and the World Wide Web

Examples here are from the World Wide Web, and a similar format can be used to cite gopher or ftp sources with the medium and path adequately identified.

Journal

>   Klein, D. F. (1997) . Control groups in pharmacotherapy and psychotherapy evaluations. Treatment, 1. Retrieved February 9, 1998 from the World Wide Web: http://journals.apa.org/treatment/vol1/97_a1.html

Newspaper article

>   Freiberg, P. (1998, February). We know how to stop the spread of AIDS: So why can't we? Psychologists point to a need for more work in the policy arena. APA Monitor [Newspaper, selected stories online.]

Retrieved February 9, 1998 from the World Wide
Web: http://www.apa.org/monitor/aids.html

Abstract

    McCutchen, A., Francis, M., & Kerr, S.
(1997). Revising for meaning: Effects of knowledge
and strategy [Abstract]. Journal of Educational
Psychology 89, 667-676. Retrieved February 9, 1998
from the World Wide Web: http://www.apa.
org/journals/edu/1297ab.html#8

22. Online abstract

    Brindelstein, C., & Chen, S. (1993). The
social interaction of small children in task
differentiated groups. [Online]. Childhood
Socializing, 14, 234-241. Abstract from:
DIALOG File: PyscINFO Item: 46-12144.

23. Online journal, subscriber-based

    Cross-Cultural Speech Interference Study
Group. (1995, October 21). Signaling
affirmation in informal conversation:
Contrasting behaviors of Hispanics and
African-Americans [720 paragraphs]. Online
Journal of Contrastive Cultural Behaviors
[Online serial]. Available: Doc. No. 99

24. Electronic database

    Survey of Public Response to Terrorism
Abroad: 1992-93. [Electronic database].
(1994). Washington, DC: Center for Public
Policy Study [Producer and Distributor].

25. CD-ROM

    Culrose, P., Trimmer, N., & Debruikker,
K. (1996). Gender differentiation in fear
responses [CD-ROM]. Emotion and Behavior, 27,
914-937. Abstract from: FirstSearch: PsycLit
Item: 900312.

26. Computer program or software

    Gangnopahdhav, A. (1994). Data analyzer
for e-mail usage [Computer software].
Princeton, NJ: MasterMinders.

Other Sources

27. Information service

Mead, J. V. (1992). Looking at old photographs: Investigating the teacher tales that novice teachers bring with them (Report No. NCRTL-RR-92-4). East Lansing, MI: National Center for Research on Teacher Learning. (ERIC Document Reproduction Service No. ED 346 082)

28. Dissertation abstract

Rosen, P. R. (1994). Learning to cope with family crises through counselor mediation (Doctoral dissertation, Clairemont University, 1994). Dissertation Abstracts International, 53, Z6812.

29. Government document

United States Bureau of Statistics. (1994). Population density in the contiguous United States (No. A1994-2306). Washington, DC: U.S. Government Printing Office.

30. Conference proceedings

Cordulla, F. M. , Teitelman, P. J. , & Preba, E. E. (1995). Bio-feedback in muscle relaxation. Proceedings of the National Academy of Biological Sciences, USA, 96, 1271–1342.

31. Interview

Personal interviews are not included in the reference list. Instead use a parenthetical citation in the text. List published interviews under the interviewer's name.

Daly, C. C. (1995, July 14). [Interview with Malcolm Forbes]. International Business Weekly, 37, 34–35.

32. Film, videotape, performance, or artwork

Start with the name and, in parentheses, functions of the originators or primary contributors; put the medium, such as film, videotape, or slides in brackets after the title; give the name and location of the distributor, and if the company is not well known, include the address.

Weiss, I. (Producer), & Terris, A. (Director). (1992). Infant babbling and speech production [Film]. (Available from Childhood Research Foundation, 125 Marchmont Avenue, Suite 224, New York, NY 10022).

33. Recording

Totonn, R. (1993). When I wander [Recorded by A. Lopper, T. Seagrim, & E. Post]. On Songs of our age [CD]. Wilmington, ME: Folk Heritage Records.

34. Cassette recording

Trussler, R. W., Jr. (Speaker). (1989). Validity of mental measurements with young children (Cassette Recording No. 21-47B). Washington, DC: American Psychological Measurements Society.

35. Television broadcast, series, and single episode from a series

Widener, I. [Executive Producer]. (1995, October 21). Window on the world. New York: Public Policy Broadcasting.

Biaccio, R. (Producer). (1994). The mind of man. New York: WNET.

Nostanci, L. (1994). The human sense of curiosity (R. Mindlin, Director). In R. Biaccio (Producer), The mind of man, New York: WNET

36. Unpublished paper presented at a meeting

Lillestein, M. A. (1994, January). Notes on inter-racial conflict in college settings. Paper presented at the meeting of the American Cultural Studies Society, San Antonio, TX.

Sample pages from an APA-style research paper

If you are using APA style and asked to include a title page, follow the format shown here for a title page. Included also

are a first page and a first page for the References list. For
all pages leave a margin of at least one inch on all sides.

1. Sample title page following APA style

(abbreviated title;   Militia Organizations   1
page numbering begins
on first page)

              1/2″

                              Militia Organizations: *(title)*

                          Their Attractions and Appeal
(center
and double-   Leila Koach   *(name)*
space)
                                 Prof. McIver   *(instructor)*

                              Humanities 204   *(course)*

                              March 22, 1999   *(date)*

2. Sample first page following APA style

Note that margins shown are adjusted to fit space limitations of book. Follow actual dimensions shown and your instructor's directions.

Militia Organizations: Their
Attractions and Appeal

As the number of militia organizations continues to increase (Billman, R. T., 1995), their members are being studied to learn more about the attraction of such groups. A number of factors have surfaced in such interviews. R. Rudner (1994) finds that the publicity surrounding such groups gives meaning to the lives of the members. Other studies (Lattner, 1994; Mukiyama, 1993; Tobias & Klein, 1994) focus on the feelings of frustration expressed by militia members who typically work in jobs that keep them in lower socioeconomic groups. The research project completed by R. Mintz and A. H. Prumanyhuma (1995) indicates that a major attraction of militia groups is their ability to provide members with a strong sense of belonging. These people, who often express accompanying feelings of alienation from society, typically have trouble fitting in elsewhere, a trait noted in several studies (Mukiyama, 1993; Tobias & Klein, 1994). P. Jukan's study (1995) reveals another dimension to the appeal of militias, their announced interest in "getting the government off their backs" (p. 121). A discussion of the results of these *(double-space)* studies will provide a profile of typical militia members and their motivations for joining these organizations.

When members profess allegiance to the goals of organizations, they are also giving significance to lives that may otherwise have little meaning. Rudner (1994) cites comments by members of the militias that indicate how their lives took on new meaning and purpose when they dedicated themselves to the work of their groups. This sense of assuming a larger goal is mentioned by Jukan (1995) but is not credited as being a major force in group commitment. However, as Bryan Liftner, the chair of a recent government task force on terrorism, notes, "allegiance to a

3. Sample References page following APA style

References

Billman, R. T. (1995, April 14). Paramilitary groups on the increase. American Public Policy, 21, 47–53.

Calmanov, K., Messer, P. B., & Nocatio, L. (1993). Public Response to Terrorism: 1992–93. [Electronic database]. (1994). Washington, DC: Center for Public Policy Study [Producer and Distributor].

Defense responses of paramilitary groups. (1991). (Report No. 27). Washington, DC: National Crime Prevention Research Project.

Farmer, P. L., Melson, W. W., & Audati, C. J. (1998). Threatening behaviors exhibited by unemployed vs. underemployed individuals. Current Studies in Psycho-social Behavior, 2. Retrieved November 12, 1998 from the World Wide Web: http://www.apa.org/studies/vol2/98_a2.html

Gumper, M., & Stark, P. T. (1993). The warrior in postwar culture. New York: Mayfair.

Jukan, P. (1995). Factors contributing to anti-government organizations' threats of violence. Journal of Culture and Contemporary Society, 23, 78–103.

Liftner, B. (1994). Report on terrorism and weapon use: 1992-1993. (U.S. Senate Task Force on Terrorism Publication No. 7). Washington, DC: Government Printing Office.

Mintz, R., & Prumanyhuma, A. H. (1995). Social alienation in members of paramilitary groups (Commission on violence in America Rep. No. 45). Washington, DC: U.S. Government Printing Office.

Mukiyama, T. (1993). Socioeconomic factors in expressions of patriotism [Online]. Mental Health Journal, 32, 92-123. Abstract from: DIALOG File: PsycINFO Item: 53-10339.

R. Rudner, R. (1994). Paramilitary doctrines and personal goals, beliefs, and fears. (Rep. No. 19). New York: City University of New York, Center for the Study of Social Action.

Tamar, R., Sylman, A., Bentur, W., & Foturin, L. (1992). Paramilitary cultures in post-Vietnam America. New York: Hampton.

Tobias, C., & Klein, J. T. (1994). Socioeconomic factors in feelings of alienation. American Journal of Psychiatric Studies, 33, 256-73.

45 Other Formats

Chicago Manual of Style

In disciplines such as history and other fields of study in the humanities, the preferred style is the *Chicago Manual*. The most recent guide for this format is *The Chicago Manual of Style* (14th ed., 1993). A shorter volume on Chicago style, for student writers, is the following:

Turabian, Kate L. *A Manual for Writers of Term Papers, Theses, and Dissertations*. 6th ed. Rev. John Grossman and Alice Bennett. Chicago: U of Chicago P, 1996.

When you use *Chicago Manual* style, include (1) notes (or endnotes) to cite references in the text, and (2) a bibliography at the end of the paper to list those works referred to in the notes.

Notes in Chicago Style

Numbering in the text

- Number citations consecutively with superscript numbers ([1]) for publication information or for explanations and additional material that would interrupt the main text if inserted there.
- Put the note number at the end of the citation following the sentence punctuation with no space between the last letter or punctuation mark.

  The violence in the Raj at that time was more pronounced than it had been in the previous conflict.[4] But, as has been noted by Peter Holman, "the military police were at a loss to stem the tide of bloodshed."[5]

Placing notes

- List notes at the bottom of the page as footnotes or at the end of the essay as endnotes.

Spacing notes

- Single-space individual notes, with the first line indented five spaces.
- Double-space between notes.

Ordering the parts of notes

- Begin with the author's first name and then last name.
- Then add the title(s).
- Then include the publishing information and page numbers.

Punctuating, capitalizing, and abbreviating

- Use commas between elements, and put publishing information within parentheses.
- Include the page number, but omit the abbreviation "p." or "pp."
- Underline or italicize titles of books and periodicals.
- Capitalize titles of articles, books, and journals.
- Use quotation marks around parts of books or articles in periodicals.
- Do not abbreviate the name of the publisher.

Later notes

- The first time a source is cited, all the relevant information is included. Later citations for that source are shortened.
- For most cases, note the author's last name, then insert a comma, and then the page(s) cited, but omit "p." or "pp."
- If you cite more than one work by the same author, use a shortened form of the title.
- If you wish, use "ibid." to refer to the work in the previous note or, if the page is different, use "ibid." followed by a comma and the page number.

```
        6. Peter Holman, The History of the
Raj: Nineteenth and Twentieth Centuries (New
York: Dorset Press, 1996), 18.
        7. Holman, 34-36.
        8. Ibid., 72.
```

Bibliography in Chicago Style

- Differences between the notes and the bibliography:

  Notes have names in natural order (first name, then last name), whereas the bibliography inverts the first author's name, with last name first.

  Elements in the bibliography are separated by periods, not commas and parentheses.

```
Holman, Peter. The History of the Raj:
    Nineteenth and Twentieth Centuries. New
    York: Dorset Press, 1996.
```

- Use the title "Bibliography," but it can also be "Select Bibliography," "Works Cited," or "References."
- Start with the first line at the left margin and indent other lines in the entry. Double-space throughout.

- Include all the elements that were in the first note for that source but do not put parentheses around the publishing information.
- Underline or italicize titles of books and periodicals.
- Use quotation marks around parts of books or articles in periodicals.
- Do not abbreviate the name of the publisher.

Parts of the bibliography
(in the order they appear)

Author	full name of author(s), editor(s), and translator(s)
Title	full title, including subtitle
Editor, compiler, or translator	if any and if in addition to the author
Volume	total number of volumes if referred to as a whole
Volume number	if a single volume in the whole work is cited
Title of individual volume	if applicable
Facts of publication	city, publisher's full name, and date
Page number(s)	or volume and page number if any

Books*

1. One author

N: 1. George Frederick Abbot, <u>Israel in Europe</u> (New York: Humanities Press, 1972), 18.

B: Abbot, George Frederick. <u>Israel in Europe</u>. New York: Humanities Press, 1972.

2. Two or three authors

N: 2. A. Y. Yodfat and Y. Arnon-Channa, <u>P.L.O. Strategy and Tactics</u> (London: Croom Helm, 1981), 45.

B: Yodfat, A. Y. and Y. Arnon-Channa. <u>P.L.O. Strategy and Tactics</u>. London: Croom Helm, 1981.

3. Four or more authors

N: 3. John K. Fairbank, Edwin O. Reischauer, George Allen, and Albert Craig, <u>East Asia:</u>

*N = **Note;** *B* = **Bibliography**

EXAMPLES OF *CHICAGO*-STYLE NOTES AND BIBLIOGRAPHY

Books
1. One author
2. Two or three authors
3. Four or more authors
4. Unknown author
5. Editor or translator
6. Edition other than the first one
7. Selection or book chapter in an anthology
8. Multivolume book
9. Reference book
10. Biblical or other scriptural reference

Periodicals
11. Article in a journal paginated by volume
12. Article in a journal paginated by issue
13. Article in a magazine
14. Article in a newspaper
15. Book review

Electronic sources
16. Information service
17. Online database
18. Electronic documents
19. Computer software

Other sources
20. Government publication
21. Unpublished dissertation
22. Interview
23. Personal communication (including e-mail)
24. Film or videotape
25. Sound recording
26. Source quoted from another source

Tradition and Transformation (Boston: Houghton, Mifflin Co., 1973), 274–5.

(Chicago *style also permits giving the name of the first author followed by "et al." or "and others" with no intervening punctuation.*)

B: Fairbank, John K., Edwin O. Reischauer,
          George Allen, and Albert Craig. East
          Asia: Tradition and Transformation.
          Boston: Houghton, Mifflin, 1973.

4. Unknown author

N: 4. The Chicago Manual of Style, 14th ed.
       (Chicago: University of Chicago Press, 1993). 420.
B: The Chicago Manual of Style. 14th ed. Chicago:
          University of Chicago Press, 1993.

5. Editor or translator

N: 5. Dan Caspi, Abraham Diskin, and
       Emmanuel Gutmann, eds., The Roots of Begin's
       Success (New York: St. Martin's Press, 1984), 36.
B: Caspi, Dan, Abraham Diskin, and Emmanuel
          Gutmann, eds. The Roots of Begin's
          Success. New York: St. Martin's
          Press, 1984.

6. Edition other than the first one

N: 6. John Joseph Mathews, The Osages:
       Children of the Middle Waters, 2nd ed. (Norman:
       University of Oklahoma Press, 1963), 145–47.
B: Mathews, John Joseph. The Osages: Children
          of the Middle Waters. 2nd ed. Norman:
          University of Oklahoma Press, 1963.

7. Selection or book chapter in an anthology

N: 7. Emmanuel Anati, "The Prehistory of
       the Holy Land (Until 3200 BC)," in A History
       of the Holy Land, ed. Michael Avi-Yonah
       (Jerusalem: Jerusalem Publishing House Ltd.,
       1969), 33–41.
B: Anati, Emmanuel. "The Prehistory of
          the Holy Land (Until 3200 BC)." In A
          History of the Holy Land, edited by
          Michael Avi-Yonah. Jerusalem: The
          Jerusalem Publishing House Ltd., 1969.

8. Multivolume book

N: 8. Cao Xuequin, The Story of Stone,
       trans. David Hawkes (Harmondsworth: Penguin
       Books, 1977), 2:150–51.

B: Xuequin, Cao, <u>The Story of Stone</u>,
          translated by David Hawkes. Vol. 2.
          Harmondsworth: Penguin Books, 1977.

9. Reference book

N: 9. <u>Encyclopedia Britannica</u>, 15th ed.,
       s.v. "Henry Clay."

(Do not include the volume or page number. Instead, cite the term in the reference book under which the information is contained. Use the abbreviation "s.v." for "sub verbo," meaning "under the word.")

B: Well-known reference books are not usually
          listed in the bibliography.

10. Biblical or other scriptural reference

N: 10. Gen. 21:14–18.

(Include the book in Roman type, abbreviated with no underline or italics, chapter, and verse. No page number.)

B: Scriptural references are usually cited
          only in the notes.

Periodicals

11. Article in a journal paginated by volume

N: 11. Russell Reid, "Journals of the
       Atkinson-O'Fallon Expedition," <u>North Dakota</u>
       <u>Historical Quarterly</u> 4 (1929): 5–56.
B: Reid, Russell. "Journals of the Atkinson-
          O'Fallon Expedition." <u>North Dakota</u>
          <u>Historical Quarterly</u> 4 (1929): 5–56.

12. Article in a journal paginated by issue

N: 12. Carl Coke Rister, "The Significance
       of the Destruction of the Buffalo in the
       Southwest," <u>Southwestern Historical Society</u>
       33, no. 1 (1929): 44.
B: Rister, Carl Coke. "The Significance of the
          Destruction of the Buffalo in the
          Southwest." <u>Southwestern Historical</u>
          <u>Society</u> 33, no. 1 (1929): 44–57.

13. Article in a magazine

N: 13. Jacob Schlesinger, "Sundown," <u>The</u>
       <u>New Republic</u>, 3 August 1998, 12.

B: Schlesinger, Jacob. "Sundown." The New
       Republic, 3 August 1998, 12.

14. Article in a newspaper

N: 14. Barbara Crossette, "New U.N. Push
       to Urge Iraq to Cooperate with Inspectors,"
       New York Times, 8 August 1998, sec. A.
B: Crossette, Barbara. "New U.N. Push to Urge
       Iraq to Cooperate with Inspectors." New
       York Times, 8 August 1998, sec. A.

15. Book review

N: 15. Bernard Lewis, review of Autumn
       of Fury: The Assassination of Anwar Sadat,
       by Mohamed Heikal, New York Review of
       Books, 31 May 1984, 25–27.
B: Lewis, Bernard. Review of Autumn of Fury:
       The Assassination of Anwar Sadat, by
       Mohamed Heikal. New York Review of
       Books, 31 May 1984, 25–27.

Electronic sources

The Chicago Manual of Style recommends following the latest documentation system of the International Standards
Organization (ISO). The ISO is constructing and continues
to modify a uniform system for citing electronic documents.

16. Information service

N: 16. Linda Flower, "Diagnoses in Revision:
       The Experts' Option." Communications Design
       Center Technical Report No. 27 (Pittsburgh:
       Carnegie Mellon University, 1986), OVID,
       ERIC ED 266 464.
B: Flower, Linda. "Diagnosis in Revision: The
       Experts' Option." Communications Design
       Center Technical Report No. 27.
       Pittsburgh: Carnegie Mellon University,
       1986. OVID, ERIC ED 266 464.

17. Online database

N: 17. Pennti Aalto, "Swells of the Mongol-
       Storm around the Baltic." Acta Orientalia
       36 (Budapest, 1982): 5–15, in Bibliography
       of Asian Studies [database online] [cited
       24 August 1998]; available from OVID

Information Services, Inc., Murray, Utah,
identifier no. 19980218.232.

B: Aalto, Pennti. "Swells of the Mongol-Storm around
        the Baltic." Acta Orientalia 36 (Budapest,
        1982): 5–15. In Bibliography of Asian
        Studies [database online] [cited 24 August
        1998]. Murray, Utah: OVID Information
        Services,Inc. Identifier no. 19980218.232.

18. Electronic documents

Listserv

N: 18. John Murray, "Economic Historians
in the News," in EH.T [electronic bulletin
board] [cited 12 March 1998]); available
from EH.T@cs.muohio.edu; INTERNET.

B: Smith, John. "Economic Historians in the
        News." In EH.T[electronic bulletin
        board]. [cited 12 March 1998]. Available
        from EH.T@cs.muohio.edu; INTERNET.

Electronic journal

N: 18. Lucia Sommer, "Simon Penny's Electronic
Critique: Notes on the Politicization of Art
Against the Aestheticization of Politics,"
Cultronix 1 [electronic journal] (Pittsburgh:
Carnegie Mellon University, 1994 [cited 27
August 1998]); available from http://eserver.
org/cultronix/sommer.

B: Sommer, Lucia. "Simon Penny's Electronic
        Critique: Notes on the Politicization
        of Art Against the Aestheticization of
        Politics." Cultronix 1 [electronic journal].
        Pittsburgh: Carnegie Mellon University,
        1994 [cited 27 August 1998]. Available
        from http://eserver.org/cultronix/sommer.

19. Computer software

N: 19. CensusCounts. Ver. 2.1, Decisionmark
Corporation, Cedar Rapids, Iowa.

B: CensusCounts. Ver. 2.1. Decisionmark
        Corporation, Cedar Rapids, Iowa.

Other sources

20. Government publication

N: 20. William Lilley, The State Atlas
of Political and Cultural Diversity

(Washington, D.C.: Congressional
Quarterly, 1997), 31–45.

B: Lilley, William. <u>The State Atlas of Political</u>
        <u>and Cultural Diversity</u>. Washington,
        D.C.: Congressional Quarterly, 1997.

21. Unpublished dissertation

N: 21. Arnold Mayniew, "Historical
Perceptions of Royal Prerogative" (Ph.D.
diss., University of Illinois, 1991), 32–37.

B: Mayniew, Arnold. "Historical Perceptions of
        Royal Prerogative."Ph.D. diss.,
        University of Illinois, 1991.

22. Interview

N: 22. David Gergen, interview by Ted
Koppell, <u>Nightline</u>, American Broadcasting
Company, 18 August 1998.

B: Gergen, David. Interview by Ted Koppell.
        <u>Nightline</u>. American Broadcasting
        Company, 18 August 1998.

23. Personal communication (including e-mail)

N: 23. Maynard Jimmerson, telephone interview
by author, 27 July 1998.

N: 24. Daniel Kaplan, e-mail to author,
15 September 1998.

B: Personal communications are not usually
       included in the bibliography.

24. Film or videotape

N: 25. <u>The Luttrell Psalter: Everyday</u>
<u>Life in Medieval England</u>, prod. and dir.
Martin Shuman, 1 hr. 22 min., Films for the
Humanities & Sciences, 1996, videocassette.

B: <u>The Luttrell Psalter: Everyday Life in Medieval</u>
        <u>England</u>. Produced and directed by Martin
        Shuman. 1 hr. 22 min. Films for the
        Humanities & Sciences, 1996. Videocassette.

25. Sound recording

N: 26. J. S. Bach, <u>Four Concerti for</u>
<u>Various Instruments</u>, Orchestra of St.
Luke's, Michael Feldman, Musical Heritage
Society, Inc. compact disk 512268T.

B: Bach, J. S. <u>Four Concerti for Various
        Instruments</u>. Orchestra of St. Luke's.
        Michael Feldman. Musical Heritage
        Society,Inc. compact disk 512268T.

26. Source quoted from another source

N: 27. H. H. Dubs, "An Ancient Chinese
    Mystery Cult," <u>Harvard Theological Review</u>,
    35 (1942): 223, quoted in Susan Naquin,
    <u>Millenarian Rebellion in China: The Eight
    Trigrams Uprising of 1813</u> (New Haven and
    London: Yale University Press, 1976), 288.

B: Dubs, H. H. "An Ancient Chinese Mystery Cult."
        <u>Harvard Theological Review</u>, 35 (1942):
        223. Quoted in Susan Naquin, <u>Millenarian
        Rebellion in China: The Eight Trigrams
        Uprising of 1813</u> (New Haven and London:
        Yale University Press, 1976), 288.

CBE (Council of Biology Editors)

Writers in the physical sciences and life sciences follow the
documentation style developed by the Council of Biology
Editors (CBE) and found in *Scientific Style and Format: The
CBE Manual for Authors, Editors, and Publishers.* 6th ed.
New York: Cambridge UP, 1994. Mathematicians use either
this style or the style in the book listed in 45, under the entry for "Mathematics." (Section 45 also has style manuals for
other scientific fields.)

The CBE Style Manual offers two documentation styles,
and you can ask your instructor which one is preferred for
your papers. Or you can check a current journal in the field.
The two styles are as follows:

1. Authors' names and publication dates

Here, authors' names and publication dates are included in
parenthetical citations in the text, closely resembling the
APA style (see section 44).

In-text citation:

   The earlier studies done on this virus (Fong
   and Townes 1992; Mindlin 1994) reported similar
   results. However, one of these studies (Mindlin
   1994) noted a mutated strain.

In the References list at the end, the names are listed alphabetically with the date after the name.

References list:

```
Fong L, Townes HC. (1992). Viral longevity.
Biological Reports 27: 129-45.
```

2. In-text numbered references

In this format, references are listed with in-text superscript numbers (numbers set above the line, such as [1] and [2]) that refer to a list of numbered references at the end. The references are numbered according to the order in which they are used in the text, and later references to the same work use the original number. When you have two or more sources cited at once, put the numbers in sequence and separate them with commas but no spaces.

In-text citation:

```
The earlier studies done on this virus[1,4,9]
reported similar results. However, one of
these studies[4] noted a mutated strain.
```

In the references at the end, list the entries in numerical order, according to the order in which they are cited in the paper, not alphabetically.

References list:

```
1. Fong L, Townes H. Viral longevity.
   Biological Reports 1992; 27: 129-45.
```

CBE References List

At the end of the paper, include a list entitled "References" (or "Cited References"). The placement of the date will differ, depending on which format you use.

Name and publication date format

■ Put the date after the author's name.

■ Arrange the list alphabetically by last names.

■ Do not indent any lines in the entries.

In-text numbered references

■ Put the date after the publisher's name for books.

■ Put the date after the periodical name for references to periodicals.

■ Arrange the list by number.

■ Put the number at the left margin, followed by the authors' last names. For the second and following lines, align beneath the first letter of the line above.

```
1. xxxxxxxxxxxxxxxxxx
   xxxxxxxxxx

2. xxxxxxxxxxxxxxxxxx
   xxxx
```

Parts of the reference
(Use periods between major divisions of the entry)

Author	-Start with last name first, no comma, and initials without periods for first and middle names. Separate authors' names with commas. End the list of authors' names with a period.
Title	-For books and article titles, use capitals only for the first word and proper nouns. No underline, italics, or quotation marks. For journals, abbreviate titles and capitalize all major words.
Place of publication (colon), publisher (semicolon), and publication date (period)	-Include a space between the full name of the publisher and date. Use a semicolon with no space between the date and volume number of the journal. Abbreviate months.
Number of pages	-For books, include the total number of pages in the book, with a space and then a "p" after the number. End the entry with a period. For journal articles, show the total number of pages of the article, and for the second number use only numbers not already included in the first number (for example: 122–7; 49–51; 131–8; 200–9). End with a period.

1. Books with one author

Glenn EP. Encyclopedia of environmental biology. San Diego: Academic Press; 1995. 1289 p.

2. Books with more than one author

Rouse Ball WW, Coxeter HSM. Mathematical recreations and essays. 13th ed. Mineola, NY: Dover Publications; 1987. 381 p.

EXAMPLES OF CBE FORMAT FOR REFERENCE LIST

1. Books with one author

2. Books with more than one author

3. Books with an editor

4. Organization as author

5. Section of a book

6. Article in scholarly journal

7. Newspaper or magazine article

8. Article with no author

9. Editorial

10. Audio-visual materials

11. Electronic journal articles

12. Web sources

3. Books with an editor

Estes JW, Smith BG, editors. A melancholy
scene of devastation: the public response to
the 1793 Philadelphia yellow fever epidemic.
Philadelphia: Science History
Publications/USA; 1997. 436 p.

4. Organization as author

Council of Biology Editors. Scientific style
and format: the CBE manual for authors,
editors, and publishers. 6th ed. New York:
Cambridge UP; 1994. 704 p.

5. Section of a book

Saari JC. Retinoids in photosensitive
systems. In: Sporn MB, editor. The

retinoids. 2nd ed. New York: Raven Press:
1994. p. 351-78.

6. Article in scholarly journal

Adleman LM. Molecular computation of
solutions to combinatorial problems. Science
1994;266:1021-4.

7. Newspaper or magazine article

Allen A. Mighty mice: the perils of patenting
genes. The New Republic 1998 Aug 10; 16-8.

8. Article with no author

Begin the entry with "[Anonymous]."

9. Editorial

After the title, add "[editorial]."

10. Audiovisual materials

The CBE Manual does not have guidelines for CD-ROM
sources, but the format shown here is a suggested model
to follow.

Recent developments in DNA models
[videocassette]. Miletius T, editor.
DistanceED Productions, producer. [San
Diego]: Media Forum; 1997. 3 videocassettes:
315 min, sound, color, 1/2 in. (Genetics
laboratories; Nr 9). Accompanied by: 3 guides.
Available from: Boston National Visual
Instruction Library, Boston, MA.

11. Electronic journal articles

Arlinghaus SL, Drake WD, Nystuen, JD.
Animaps. Solstice: an electronic journal of
geography and mathematics 1998;9(1):
Available from: http://www-personal.umich.
edu/~sarhaus/image/animaps.html. Accessed
1998 Aug 16.

12. Web sources

The CBE Manual does not have guidelines for citing Web
sources. The following suggested format follows the journal

article format and includes the date of Internet publication, the Web address, and your date of access.

> Finn R. DNA vaccines generate excitement as human trials begin. The Scientist 1998 Mar.16; 12(16):http://www.the-scientist. library.upenn.edu/yr1998/mar/research_980316 .html. Accessed 1998 Aug 16.

Style manuals for various fields

Anthropology
Uses *Chicago Manual of Style* (see page 189) and *Webster's 10th New Collegiate Dictionary.*

On its Web site the American Anthropological Association offers a brief "AAA Style Guide" : http://www.ameranthassn.org/aaastyle.htm#1

Astronomy
See entry for **Physics.**

Biology
Council of Biology Editors. *Scientific Style and Format: The CBE Manual for Authors, Editors, and Publishers.* 6th ed. New York: Cambridge UP, 1994.

Chemistry
Dodd, Janet S., ed. *The ACS Style Guide: A Manual for Authors and Editors.* 2nd ed. Washington: Amer. Chemical Soc., 1997.

Education
Uses APA (see section 44) and MLA (see section 43).

English
Gibaldi, Joseph, and Walter S. Achert. *MLA Handbook for Writers of Research Papers.* 5th ed. New York: Modern Language Association of America, 1999.
(See section 43.)

History
Uses *Chicago Manual of Style,* 14th edition. Chicago: U of Chicago P, 1993.
(See page 189.)

Journalism
Goldstein, Norm, et al. *Associated Press Style Book and Libel Manual.* Rev. and updated Ed. Portland: Perseus Press, 1998.

Lewis, Jordan, ed. *New York Times Manual of Style and Usage.* New York: Times Books, 1982.

Mathematics

American Mathematical Society. *The AMS Author Handbook: General Instructions for Preparing Manuscripts.* Providence: AMS, 1997.

Medicine

Iverson, Cheryl, et al. *American Medical Association Manual of Style.* 9th ed. Baltimore: Williams and Wilkins, 1997.

Music

Holoman, D. Kern, ed. *Writing about Music: A Style Sheet from the Editors of 19th-Century Music.* Berkeley: U of California P, 1988.

Philosophy

Guidebook for Publishing in Philosophy. Newark, DE: American Philosophy Association, 1997.

Physics and Astronomy

American Institute of Physics. *AIP Style Manual.* 4th ed. College Park, MD: AIP, 1990.

Political Science

American Political Science Association. *Style Manual for Political Science.* Washington: Amer. Political Science Assn., 1984.

Psychology

American Psychological Association. *Publication Manual of the American Psychological Association.* 4th ed. Washington: APA, 1994.
(See section 44.)

Glossary of Usage

This list includes words and phrases you may be uncertain about when writing. If you have questions about words not included here, try the index at the back of this book to see whether the word is discussed elsewhere. You can also check a recently published dictionary.

A, An Use *a* before words beginning with a consonant and before words beginning with a vowel that sounds like a consonant:

a cat   a house   a one-way street   a union   a history

Use *an* before words that begin with a vowel and before words with a silent *h*.

an egg   an ice cube   an hour   an honor

Accept, Except *Accept,* a verb, means to agree to, to believe, or to receive.

The detective **accepted** his account of the event.

Except, a verb, means to exclude or leave out, and *except,* a preposition, means leaving out.

Because he did not know the answers, he was **excepted** from the list of contestants and asked to leave.

Except for brussel sprouts, I eat most vegetables.

Advice, Advise *Advice* is a noun, and *advise* is a verb.

She always offers too much **advice.**

Would you **advise** me about choosing the right course?

Affect, Effect Most frequently, *affect,* which means to influence, is used as a verb, and *effect,* which means a result, is used as a noun.

The weather **affects** my ability to study.

What **effect** does coffee have on your concentration?

However, *effect,* meaning to cause or bring about, is also used as a verb.

The new traffic enforcement laws **effected** a change in people's driving habits.

Common phrases with *effect* include the following:

in effect   to that effect

Ain't This is a nonstandard way of saying *am not, is not, has not, have not,* and so on.

All Ready, Already *All ready* means *prepared*; *already* means *before* or *by this time.*

The courses for the meal are **all ready** to be served.

When I got home, she was **already** there.

All Right, Alright *All right* is two words, not one. *Alright* is an incorrect form.

All Together, Altogether *All together* means *in a group,* and *altogether* means *entirely, totally.*

> We were **all together** again after having separate vacations.

> He was not **altogether** happy about the outcome of the test.

Alot, A Lot *Alot* is an incorrect form of *a lot.*

a.m., p.m. (or) A.M., P.M. Use these with numbers, not as substitutes for the words *morning* or *evening.*

> *morning at 9 a.m.*
> We meet every ~~a.m.~~ for an exercise class.

Among, Between Use *among* when referring to three or more things and *between* when referring to two things.

> The decision was discussed **among** all the members of the committee.

> I had to decide **between** the chocolate mousse pie and the almond ice cream.

Amount, Number Use *amount* for things or ideas that are general or abstract and cannot be counted. For example, furniture is a general term and cannot be counted. That is, we cannot say *one furniture* or *two furnitures.* Use *number* for things that can be counted (for example, *four chairs* or *three tables*).

> He had a huge **amount** of work to finish before the deadline.

> There were a **number** of people who saw the accident.

An See the entry for **a, an.**

And Although some people discourage the use of *and* as the first word in a sentence, it is an acceptable word with which to begin a sentence.

And Etc. Adding *and* is redundant because *et* means *and* in Latin. See the entry for **etc.**

Anybody, Any Body See the entry for **anyone, any one.**

Anyone, Any One *Anyone* means *any person at all. Any one* refers to a specific person or thing in a group. There are similar distinctions for other words ending in *-body* and *-one* (for example, *everybody, every body, anybody, any body, someone,* and *some one*).

> The teacher asked if **anyone** knew the answer.

> **Any one** of those children could have taken the ball.

Anyways, Anywheres These are nonstandard forms for *anyway* and *anywhere.*

As, As if, As Though, Like Use *as* in a comparison (not *like*) when there is an equality intended or when the meaning is *in the function of.*

> Celia acted **as** [not *like*] the leader when the group was getting organized.   (Celia = leader)

Use *as if* or *as though* for the subjunctive.

He spent his money **as if** [or **as though**] he were rich.

Use *like* in a comparison (not *as*) when the meaning is *in the manner of* or *to the same degree as.*

The boy swam **like** a fish.

Don't use *like* as the opening word in a clause in formal writing:

Informal: **Like** I thought, he was unable to predict the weather.

Formal: **As** I thought, he was unable to predict the weather.

Assure, Ensure, Insure *Assure* means *to declare or promise, ensure* means *to make safe or certain,* and *insure* means *to protect with a contract of insurance.*

I **assure** you that I am trying to find your lost package.

Some people claim that eating properly **ensures** good health.

This insurance policy also **insures** my car against theft.

Awful, Awfully *Awful* is an adjective meaning *inspiring awe* or *extremely unpleasant.*

He was involved in an **awful** accident.

Awfully is an adverb used in very informal writing to mean *very.* Avoid it in formal writing.

Informal: The dog was **awfully** dirty.

Awhile, A While *Awhile* is an adverb meaning *a short time* and modifies a verb:

He talked **awhile** and then left.

A while is an article with the noun *while* and means *a period of time*:

I'll be there in **a while.**

Bad, Badly *Bad* is an adjective and is used after linking verbs. *Badly* is an adverb. (See section 15.)

The wheat crop looked **bad** [not *badly*] because of lack of rain.

There was a **bad** flood last summer.

The building was **badly** constructed and unable to withstand the strong winds.

Beside, Besides *Beside* is a preposition meaning *at the side of, compared with,* or *having nothing to do with. Besides* is a preposition meaning *in addition to* or *other than. Besides* as an adverb means *also* or *moreover.* Don't confuse *beside* with *besides.*

That is **beside** the point.

Besides the radio, they had no other means of contact with the outside world.

Besides, I enjoyed the concert.

Between, Among See the entry for **among, between.**

Breath, Breathe *Breath* is a noun, and *breathe* is a verb.

> She held her **breath** when she dived into the water.

> Learn to **breathe** deeply when you swim.

But Although some people discourage the use of *but* as the first word in a sentence, it is an acceptable word with which to begin a sentence.

Can, May *Can* is a verb that expresses *ability, knowledge,* or *capacity*:

> He **can** play both the violin and the cello.

May is a verb that expresses possibility or permission. Careful writers avoid using *can* to mean permission:

> **May** [not *can*] I sit here?

Can't Hardly This is incorrect because it is a double negative.

> She ~~can't~~ hardly hear normal voice levels.
> *can*

Choose, Chose *Choose* is the present tense of the verb, and *chose* is the past tense:

> Jennie should **choose** strawberry ice cream.

> Yesterday, she **chose** strawberry-flavored popcorn.

Cite, Site *Cite* is a verb that means *to quote an authority or source*; *site* is a noun referring to a place.

> Be sure to **cite** your sources in the paper.

> That is the **site** of the new city swimming pool.

Cloth, Clothe *Cloth* is a noun, and *clothe* is a verb.

> Here is some **cloth** for a new scarf.

> His paycheck helps to feed and **clothe** many people in his family.

Compared to, Compared with Use *compared to* when showing that two things are alike. Use *compared with* when showing similarities and differences.

> The speaker **compared** the economy **to** a roller coaster because both have sudden ups and downs.

> The detective **compared** the fingerprints **with** other sets from a previous crime.

Could of This is incorrect. Instead use *could have.*

Data This is the plural form of *datum*. In informal usage, *data* is used as a singular noun, with a singular verb. However, because dictionaries do not accept this, use *data* as a plural form for academic writing.

Informal Usage: The **data** is inconclusive.
Formal Usage: The **data** are inconclusive.

Different from, Different than *Different from* is always correct, but some writers use *different than* if a clause follows this phrase.

This program is **different from** the others.

That is a **different** result **than** they predicted.

Done The past tense forms of the verb *do* are *did* and *done*. *Did* is the simple form that needs no additional verb as a helper. *Done* is the past form that requires the helper *have*. Some writers make the mistake of interchanging *did* and *done*.

did
They ~~done~~ it again.   (or)   have
They done it again.

Effect, Affect See the entry for **affect, effect.**

Ensure See the entry for **assure, ensure, insure.**

Etc. This is an abbreviation of the Latin *et cetera,* meaning *and the rest.* Because it should be used sparingly if at all in formal academic writing, substitute other phrases such as *and so forth* or *and so on.*

Everybody, Every Body See the entry for **anyone, any one.**

Everyone, Every One See the entry for **anyone, any one.**

Except, Accept See the entry for **accept, except.**

Farther, Further Although some writers use these words interchangeably, dictionary definitions differentiate them. *Farther* is used when actual distance is involved, and *further* is used to mean *to a greater extent, more.*

The house is **farther** from the road than I realized.

That was **furthest** from my thoughts at the time.

Fewer, Less *Fewer* is used for things that can be counted (*fewer trees, fewer people*), and *less* is used for ideas, abstractions, things that are thought of collectively, not separately (*less trouble, less furniture*), and things that are measured by amount, not number (*less milk, less fuel*).

Fun This noun is used informally as an adjective.

Informal: They had a **fun** time.

Goes, Says *Goes* is a nonstandard form of *says.*

says
Whenever I give him a book to read, he ~~goes~~, "What's it about?"

Gone, Went Past tense forms of the verb *go. Went* is the simple form that needs no additional verb as a helper. *Gone* is the past form that requires the helper *have.* Some writers make the mistake of interchanging *went* and *gone.* (See section 13.)

went (or) have gone
They ~~gone~~ away yesterday.

Good, Well *Good* is an adjective and therefore describes only nouns. *Well* is an adverb and therefore describes adjectives, other adverbs, and verbs. The word *well* is used as an adjective only in the sense of *in good health*. (See section 15.)

The stereo works ~~good~~. *well* I feel ~~good~~. *well*

She is a **good** driver.

Got, Have *Got* is the past tense of *get* and should not be used in place of *have*. Similarly, *got to* should not be used as a substitute for *must*. *Have got to* is an informal substitute for *must*.

Do you ~~got~~ *have* any pennies for the meter?

I ~~got to~~ *must* go now.

Informal: You have **got to** see that movie.

Great This adjective is overworked in its formal meaning of *very enjoyable, good,* or *wonderful* and should be reserved for its more exact meanings such as *of remarkable ability, intense, high degree of,* and so on.

Informal: That was a **great** movie.

More exact uses of *great:*

The vaccine was a **great** discovery.

The map went into **great** detail.

Have, Got See the entry for **got, have.**

Have, Of *Have,* not *of,* should follow verbs such as *could, might, must,* and *should.*

They should ~~of~~ *have* called by now.

Hisself This is a nonstandard substitute for *himself.*

Hopefully This adverb means *in a hopeful way.* Many people consider the meaning *it is to be hoped* as unacceptable.

Acceptable: He listened **hopefully** for the knock at the door.

Often considered

unacceptable: **Hopefully,** it will not rain tonight.

I Although some people discourage the use of *I* in formal essays, it is acceptable. If you wish to eliminate the use of *I,* see section 7 on passive verbs.

Imply, Infer Some writers use these interchangeably, but careful writers maintain the distinction between the two words. *Imply* means *to suggest without stating directly, to hint. Infer* means *to reach an opinion from facts or reasoning.*

The tone of her voice **implied** he was stupid.

The anthropologist **inferred** this was a burial site for prehistoric people.

Insure See the entry for **assure, ensure, insure.**

Irregardless This is an incorrect form of the word *regardless.*

Is When, Is Why, Is Where, Is Because These are incorrect forms for definitions. See section 6 and the Glossary of Grammatical Terms on faulty predication.

Faulty predication:	Nervousness is when my palms sweat.
Revised:	When I am nervous, my palms sweat.
	(or)
	Nervousness is a state of being very uneasy or agitated.

Its, It's *Its* is a personal pronoun in the possessive case. *It's* is a contraction for *it is.*

The kitten licked **its** paw.

It's a good time for a vacation.

Kind, Sort These two forms are singular and should be used with *this* or *that.* Use *kinds* or *sorts* with *these* or *those.*

This **kind** of cloud indicates heavy rain.

These **sorts** of plants are regarded as weeds.

Lay, Lie *Lay* is a verb that needs an object and should not be used in place of *lie,* a verb that takes no direct object. (See section 13.)

He should ~~lay~~ lie down and rest awhile.

You can ~~lie~~ lay that package on the front table.

Leave, Let *Leave* means *to go away,* and *let* means *to permit.* It is incorrect to use *leave* when you mean *let:*

~~Leave~~ Let me get that for you.

Less, Fewer See the entry for **fewer, less.**

Let, Leave See the entry for **leave, let.**

Like, As See the entry for **as, as if, like.**

Like for The phrase "I'd like *for* you to do that" is incorrect. Omit *for.*

May, Can See the entry for **can, may.**

Most It is incorrect to use *most* as a substitute for *almost.*

Nowheres This is an incorrect form of *nowhere.*

Number, Amount See the entry for **amount, number.**

Of, Have See the entry for **have, of.**

Off of It is incorrect to write *off of* for *off* in a phrase such as *off the table*.

O.K., Ok, Okay These can be used informally but should not be used in formal or academic writing.

Reason . . . Because This is redundant. Instead of *because*, use *that*:

> The reason she dropped the course is ~~because~~ ^{*that*} she couldn't keep up with the homework.

Less wordy revision: She dropped the course **because** she couldn't keep up with the homework.

Reason Why Using *why* is redundant. Drop the word *why*.

> The reason ~~why~~ I called is to remind you of your promise.

Saw, Seen Past tense forms of the verb *see. Saw* is the simple form that needs no additional verb as a helper. *Seen* is the past form that requires the helper *have*. Some writers make the mistake of interchanging *saw* and *seen*. (See section 13.)

> They ~~seen~~ ^{*saw*} it happen. (or) They _^ seen it happen. ^{*have*}

Set, Sit *Set* means *to place* and is followed by a direct object. *Sit* means *to be seated*. It is incorrect to substitute *set* for *sit*.

> Come in and ~~set~~ ^{*sit*} down.

> ~~Sit~~ ^{*Set*} the flowers on the table.

Should of This is incorrect. Instead use *should have*.

Sit, Set See the entry for **set, sit**.

Site, Cite See the entry for **cite, site**.

Somebody, Some Body See the entry for **anyone, any one**.

Someone, Some One See the entry for **anyone, any one**.

Sort, Kind See the entry for **kind, sort**.

Such This is an overworked word when used in place of *very or extremely*.

Suppose to, Use to These are nonstandard forms for *supposed to* and *used to*.

Sure The use of *sure* as an adverb is informal. Careful writers use *surely* instead.

Informal: I **sure** hope you can join us.

Revised: I **surely** hope you can join us.

Than, Then *Than* is a conjunction introducing the second element in comparison. *Then* is an adverb meaning *at that time, next, after that, also*, or *in that case*.

She is taller **than** I am.

He picked up the ticket and **then** left the house.

That There, This Here, These Here, Those There These are incorrect forms for *that, this, these, those.*

That, Which Use *that* for essential clauses and *which* for nonessential clauses. Some writers, however, also use *which* for essential clauses. (See section 19.)

Their, There, They're *Their* is a possessive pronoun; *there* means *in, at,* or *to that place*; and *they're* is a contraction for *they are.*

Their house has been sold.

There is the parking lot.

They're both good swimmers.

Theirself, Theirselves, Themself These are all incorrect forms for *themselves.*

Them It is incorrect to use this in place of either the pronoun *these* or *those.*

Look at ~~them~~ *those* apples.

Then, Than See the entry for **than, then.**

Thusly This is an incorrect substitute for *thus.*

To, Too, Two *To* is a preposition; *Too* is an adverb meaning *very* or *also*; and *two* is a number.

He brought his bass guitar **to** the party.

He brought his drums **too.**

He had **two** music stands.

Toward, Towards Both are accepted forms with the same meaning although *toward* is preferred in American usage.

Use to This is incorrect for the modal meaning *formerly.* Instead, use *used to.*

Use to, Suppose to See the entry for **suppose to, use to.**

Want for Omit the incorrect *for* in phrases such as "I want *for* you to come here."

Well, Good See the entry for **good, well.**

Went, Gone See the entry for **gone, went.**

Where It is incorrect to use *where* to mean *when* or *that.*

The Fourth of July is a holiday ~~where~~ *when* the town council shoots off fireworks.

I see ~~where~~ *that* there is now a ban on shooting panthers.

Where . . . at This is a redundant form. Omit *at.*

This is where the picnic is ~~at~~.

Which, That See the entry for **that, which.**

While, Awhile See the entry for **awhile, a while.**

Who, Whom Use *who* for the subject case; use *whom* for the object case.

> He is the person **who** signs that form.

> He is the person **whom** I asked for help.

Who's, Whose *Who's* is a contraction for *who is; whose* is a possessive pronoun.

> **Who's** included on that list?

> **Whose** wristwatch is this?

Your, You're *Your* is a possessive pronoun; *you're* is a contraction for *you are.*

> **Your** hands are cold.

> **You're** a great success.

 # Glossary of Grammatical Terms

Absolutes Words or phrases that modify whole sentences rather than parts of sentences or individual words. An absolute phrase, which consists of a noun and participle, can be placed anywhere in the sentence but needs to be set off from the sentence by commas.

> **The snow having finally stopped,** the football
> (absolute phrase)
> game began.

Abstract Nouns Nouns that refer to ideas, qualities, generalized concepts, and conditions and do not have plural forms. (See section 31.)

> happiness, pride, furniture, trouble, sincerity

Active Voice See **Voice.**

Adjectives Words that modify nouns and pronouns. (See section 15.)

Descriptive adjectives (*red, clean, beautiful, offensive,* for example) have three forms:

Positive:	red, clean, beautiful, offensive
Comparative (for comparing two things):	cleaner, more beautiful, less offensive
Superlative (for comparing more than two things):	cleanest, most beautiful, least offensive

Adjective Clauses See **Dependent Clauses.**

Adverbs Modify verbs, verb forms, adjectives, and other adverbs. (See section 15.) Descriptive adverbs (for example, *fast, graceful, awkward*) have three forms:

Positive:	fast, graceful, awkward
Comparative (for comparing two things):	faster, more graceful, less awkward
Superlative (for comparing more than two things):	fastest, most graceful, least awkward

Adverb Clauses See **Dependent Clauses.**

Agreement The use of the corresponding form for related words in order to have them agree in number, person, or gender. (See sections 13 and 14.)

John runs. (Both subject and verb are singular.)

It is necessary to flush the **pipes** regularly so that **they** don't freeze.

(Both subjects, *it* and *they,* are in third person; *they* agrees in number with the antecedent, *pipes.*)

Antecedents Words or groups of words to which pronouns refer.

When the **bell** was rung, **it** sounded very loudly.

(*Bell* is the antecedent of *it.*)

Antonyms Words with opposite meanings.

Word	**Antonym**
hot	cold
fast	slow
noisy	quiet

Appositives Nonessential phrases and clauses that follow nouns and identify or explain them. (See section 19.)

My uncle, **who lives in Wyoming,** is taking windsurfing
         (appositive)
lessons in Florida.

Articles See **noun determiners** and section 32.

Auxiliary Verbs Verbs used with main verbs in verb phrases.

should be going	**has** taken
(auxiliary verb)	(auxiliary verb)

Cardinal Numbers See **Noun Determiners.**

Case The form or position of a noun or pronoun that shows its use or relationship to other words in a sentence. The three cases in English are (1) subject (or subjective or nominative), (2) object (or objective), and (3) possessive (or genitive). (See section 14.)

Clauses Groups of related words that contain both subjects and predicates and function either as sentences or as parts of sentences. Clauses are either independent (or main) or dependent (or subordinate). (See section 11.)

Collective Nouns Nouns that refer to groups of people or things, such as a *committee, team,* or *jury.* When the group includes a number of members acting as a unit and is the subject of the sentence, the verb is also singular. (See section 13.)

The **jury** has made a decision.

Comma Splices Punctuation errors in which two or more independent clauses in compound sentences are separated only by commas and no coordinating conjunctions. (See section 12.)

Jessie said he could not help, *but* (or) ; that was typical of his responses to requests.

Common Nouns Nouns that refer to general rather than specific categories of people, places, and things and are not capitalized. (See section 24.)

basket, person, history, tractor

Comparative The form of adjectives and adverbs used when two things are being compared. (See section 15.)

higher, more intelligent, less friendly

Complement When linking verbs link subjects to adjectives or nouns, the adjectives or nouns are complements.

Phyllis was **tired.**
          (complement)

She became a **musician.**
                (complement)

Complex Sentences Sentences with at least one independent clause and at least one dependent clause arranged in any order.

Compound Nouns Words such as *swimming pool, dropout, roommate,* and *stepmother,* in which more than one word is needed.

Compound Sentences Sentences with two or more independent clauses and no dependent clauses. (See section 12.)

Compound-Complex Sentences Sentences with at least two independent clauses and at least one dependent clause arranged in any order.

Conjunctions Words that connect other words, phrases, and clauses in sentences. *Coordinating conjunctions* connect independent clauses; *subordinating conjunctions* connect dependent or subordinating clauses with independent or main clauses.

Coordinating Conjunctions: and, but, for, or, nor, so, yet

Some Subordinating Conjunctions: after, although, because, if, since, until, while

Conjunctive Adverbs Words that begin or join independent clauses. (See section 19.)

consequently, however, therefore, thus, moreover

Connotation   The attitudes and emotional overtones beyond the direct definition of a word.

> The words *plump* and *fat* both mean fleshy, but *plump* has a more positive connotation than *fat*.

Consistency   Maintaining the same voice with pronouns, the same tense with verbs, and the same tone, voice, or mode of discourse. (See section 17.)

Coordinating Conjunctions See **Conjunctions.**

Coordination   Of equal importance. Two independent clauses in the same sentence are coordinate because they have equal importance and the same emphasis.

Correlative Conjunctions Words that work in pairs and give emphasis.

> both . . . and   neither . . . nor   either . . . or
> not . . . but also

Dangling Modifiers Phrases or clauses in which the doer of the action is not clearly indicated. (See section 16.)

> *Tim thought*
> Missing an opportunity to study, the exam seemed especially difficult.
>   ^

Declarative Mood See **Mood.**

Demonstrative Pronouns   Pronouns that refer to things. (See **Noun Determiners.**)

> this, that, these, those

Denotation The explicit dictionary definition of a word, as opposed to the connotation of a word. (See **Connotation.**)

Dependent Clauses (Subordinate Clauses)   Clauses that cannot stand alone as complete sentences. (See section 11.) There are two kinds of dependent clauses: adverb clauses and adjective clauses.

Adverb clauses:	Begin with subordinating conjunctions such as *after, if, because, while, when.*
Adjective clauses:	Tell more about nouns or pronouns in sentences and begin with words such as *who, which, that, whose, whom.*

Determiner See **Noun Determiner.**

Diagrams See **Sentence Diagrams.**

Direct Discourse See **Mode of Discourse.**

Direct/Indirect Quotations   Direct quotations are the exact words said by someone or the exact words in print that are being copied. Indirect quotations are not the exact words but the rephrasing or summarizing of someone else's words. (See section 22.)

Direct Objects   Nouns or pronouns that follow a transitive verb and complete the meaning or receive the action of the verb. The direct object answers the question *what?* or *whom?*

Ellipsis A series of three dots to indicate that words or parts of sentences are being omitted from material being quoted. (See section 23.)

Essential and Nonessential Clauses and Phrases *Essential* (also called *restrictive*) clauses and phrases appear after nouns and are necessary or essential to complete the meaning of the sentence. *Nonessential* (also called *nonrestrictive*) clauses and phrases appear after nouns and add extra information, but that information can be removed from the sentence without altering the meaning. (See section 19.)

> Apples **that are green** are not sweet.
>
> (essential clause)

> Golden Delicious apples, **which are yellow,** are sweet.
>
> (nonessential clause)

Excessive Coordination Occurs when too many equal clauses are strung together with coordinators into one sentence.

Excessive Subordination Occurs when too many subordinate clauses are strung together in a complex sentence.

Faulty Coordination Occurs when two clauses that are either unequal in importance or that have little or no connection to each other are combined in one sentence and written as independent clauses.

Faulty Parallelism See **Parallel Construction.**

Faulty Predication Occurs when a predicate does not appropriately fit the subject. This happens most often after forms of the *to be* verb. (See section 6.)

> He
> ~~The reason he~~ was late ~~was~~ because he had to study.

Fragments Groups of words punctuated as sentences that either do not have both a subject and a complete verb or that are dependent clauses. (See section 11.)

> Whenever we wanted to pick fresh fruit while we were
> , we would head for the orchard with buckets
> staying on my grandmother's farm.

Fused Sentences Punctuation errors (also called *run-ons*) in which there is no punctuation between independent clauses in the sentence. (See section 12.)

> Jennifer never learned how to ask politely ;
> she just took what she wanted.

Gerunds Verbal forms ending in *-ing* that function as nouns. (See **Phrases** and **Verbals.**)

> Arnon enjoys **cooking.**
>
> (gerund)

> **Jogging** is another of his pastimes.
>
> (gerund)

Homonyms Words that sound alike but are spelled differently and have different meanings. (See section 28.)

> hear/here   passed/past   buy/by

Idioms Expressions meaning something beyond the simple definition or literal translation into another language. For example, idioms such as "short and sweet" or "wearing his heart on his sleeve" are expressions in English that cannot be translated literally into another language. (See section 35.)

Imperative Mood See **Mood.**

Indefinite Pronouns Pronouns that make indefinite reference to nouns.

> anyone, everyone, nobody, something

Independent Clauses Clauses that can stand alone as complete sentences because they do not depend on other clauses to complete their meanings. (See section 11.)

Indirect Discourse See **Mode of Discourse.**

Indirect Objects Words that follow transitive verbs and come before direct objects. They indicate the one to whom or for whom something is given, said, or done and answer the questions *to what?* or *to whom?* Indirect objects can always be paraphrased by a prepositional phrase beginning with *to* or *for*.

> Alice gave **me** some money.
>> (indirect object)

> **Paraphrase:**   Alice gave some money to me.

Infinitives Phrases made up of the present form of the verb preceded by *to*. Infinitives can have subjects, objects, complements, or modifiers. (See section 16.)

> Everyone wanted **to swim** in the new pool.
>> (infinitive)

Intensifiers Modifying words used for emphasis.

> She **most certainly** did fix that car!
>> (intensifiers)

Interjections Words used as exclamations.

> **Oh,** I don't think I want to know about that.
> (interjection)

Interrogative Pronouns Pronouns used in questions.

> who, whose, whom, which, that

Irregular Verbs Verbs in which the past tense forms and/or the past participles are not formed by adding *-ed* or *-d.* (See section 13.)

> do, did, done   begin, began, begun

Jargon Words and phrases that are either the specialized language of various fields or, in a negative sense, unnecessarily technical or inflated terms. (See section 5.)

Intransitive Verbs See **Verbs.**

Linking Verbs Verbs linking the subject to the subject complement. The most common linking verbs are *appear, seem, become, feel, look, taste, sound,* and *be.*

> I **feel** sleepy.   He **became** the president.
> ↗(linking verb)   ↗(linking verb)

Misplaced Modifiers Modifiers not placed next to or close to the word(s) being modified. (See section 16.)

We saw an advertisement for an excellent new stereo system with dual headphones ~~on television~~.
(on television inserted above; caret ^ after headphones)

Modal Verbs Helping verbs such as *shall, should, will, would, can, could, may, might, must, ought to,* and *used to* that express an attitude such as interest, possibility, or obligation. (See section 30.)

Mode of Discourse Direct discourse repeats the exact words that someone says, and indirect discourse reports the words but changes some of the words.

Everett said, **"I want to become a physicist."**

(direct discourse)

Everett said **that he wants to become a physicist.**

(indirect discourse)

Modifiers Words or groups of words that describe or limit other words, phrases, and clauses. The most common modifiers are adjectives and adverbs. (See section 16.)

Mood Verbs indicate whether a sentence expresses a fact (the declarative or indicative mood); expresses some doubt or something contrary to fact or states a recommendation (the subjunctive mood); or issues a command (the imperative mood).

Nonessential Clauses and Phrases See **Essential and Nonessential Clauses and Phrases.**

Nonrestrictive Clauses and Phrases See **Essential and Nonessential Clauses and Phrases.**

Nouns Words that name people, places, things, and ideas and have plural or possessive endings. Nouns function as subjects, direct objects, predicate nominatives, objects of prepositions, and indirect objects.

Noun Clauses Subordinate clauses used as nouns.

What I see here is adequate.
(noun clause)

Noun Determiners Words that signal a noun is about to follow. They stand next to their nouns or can be separated by adjectives. Some noun determiners can also function as nouns. There are five types of noun determiners:

1. Articles: definite: the; indefinite: a, an
2. Demonstratives: this, that, these, those
3. Possessives: my, our, your, his, her, its, their
4. Cardinal numbers: one, two, three, and so on
5. Miscellaneous: all, another, each, every, much, and others

Noun Phrases See **Phrases.**

Number The quantity expressed by a noun or pronoun, either singular (one) or plural (more than one).

Objects See **Direct Objects** and **Object Complements.**

Object Complements The adjectives in predicates modifying the object of the verb (not the subject).

The enlargement makes the picture **clear.**

(object complement)

Object of the Preposition Noun following the preposition. The preposition, its object, and any modifiers make up the prepositional phrase.

For **Daniel**

(object of the preposition *for*)

She knocked twice **on the big wooden door.**

(prepositional phrase)

Objective Case of Pronouns The case needed when the pronoun is the direct or indirect object of the verb or the object of a preposition.

Singular	**Plural**
First person: me	First person: us
Second person: you	Second person: you
Third person: him, her, it	Third person: them

Parallel Construction When two or more items are listed or compared, they must be in the same grammatical form as equal elements. When items are not in the same grammatical form, they lack parallel structure (often called *faulty parallelism*). (See section 8.)

She was sure that **being an apprentice in a photographer's studio** would be more useful than **being a student in photography classes.**

(The phrases in bold type are parallel because they have the same grammatical form.)

Parenthetical Elements Nonessential words, phrases, and clauses set off by commas, dashes, or parentheses.

Participles Verb forms that may be part of the complete verb or function as adjectives or adverbs. The present participle ends in *-ing,* and the past participle usually ends in *-ed, -d, -n,* or *-t.* (See **Phrases.**)

Present participles: running, sleeping, digging

She is **running** for mayor in this campaign.

(present participle)

Past participles: walked, deleted, chosen

The **elected** candidate will take office in January.

(past participle)

Parts of Speech The eight classes into which words are grouped according to their function, place, meaning, and use in a sentence: nouns, pronouns, verbs, adjectives, adverbs, prepositions, conjunctions, and interjections.

Passive Voice See **Voice.**

Past Participle See **Participles.**

Perfect Progressive Tense See **Verb Tenses.**

Perfect Tenses See **Verb Tenses.**

Person There are three "persons" in English.

First person:	the person(s) speaking I or we
Second person:	the person(s) spoken to you
Third person:	the person(s) spoken about he, she, it, they, anyone, etc.

Personal Pronouns Refer to people or things.

Singular	Subject	Object	Possessive
First person	I	me	my, mine
Second person	you	you	your, yours
Third person	he, she, it	him, her, it	his, her, hers, its

Plural	Subject	Object	Possessive
First person	we	us	our, ours
Second person	you	you	your, yours
Third person	they	them	their, theirs

Phrases Groups of related words without subjects and predicates. Verb phrases function as verbs.

She **has been eating** too much sugar.
          ↗ (verb phrase)

Noun phrases function as nouns.

A **major winter storm** hit **the eastern coast of Maine.**
  ↗ (noun phrase)   ↗ (noun phrase)

Prepositional phrases usually function as modifiers.

That book **of hers** is overdue at the library.
                    ↗ (prepositional phrase)

Participial phrases, gerund phrases, infinitive phrases, appositive phrases, and absolute phrases function as adjectives, adverbs, or nouns.

Participial Phrase:	I saw people **staring at my peculiar-looking haircut.**
Gerund Phrase:	**Making copies of videotapes** can be illegal.
Infinitive Phrase:	He likes **to give expensive presents.**
Appositive Phrase:	You ought to see Dr. Elman, **a dermatologist.**

Absolute Phrase: **The test done,** he sighed with relief.

Possessive Pronouns See **Personal Pronouns, Noun Determiners,** and section 14.

Predicate Adjectives See **Subject Complements.**

Predicate Nominatives See **Subject Complements.**

Predication Words or groups of words that express action or state of beginning in a sentence and consist of one or more verbs, plus any complements or modifiers.

Prefixes Word parts added to the beginning of words.

Prefix	Word
bio- (life)	biography
mis- (wrong, bad)	misspell

Prepositions Link and relate their objects (usually nouns or pronouns) to some other word or words in a sentence. Prepositions usually precede their objects but may follow the objects and appear at the end of the sentence.

The waiter gave the check **to my date** by mistake.

(prepositional phrase)

I wonder **what** she is asking **for.**

(object of   (preposition)
the preposition)

Prepositional Phrases See **Phrases.**

Progressive Tenses See **Verb Tenses.**

Pronouns Words that substitute for nouns. (See section 14.) Pronouns should refer to previously stated nouns, called antecedents.

When **Josh** came in, **he** brought some firewood.

(antecedent)   (pronoun)

Forms of pronouns: personal, possessive, reflexive, interrogative, demonstrative, indefinite, and relative.

Pronoun Case Refers to the form of the pronoun that is needed in a sentence. See **Subject, Object,** and **Possessive Cases** and section 14.

Proper Nouns Refer to specific people, places, and things. Proper nouns are always capitalized. (See section 24.)

Copenhagen Honda House of Representatives Spanish

Reflexive Pronouns Pronouns that show someone or something in the sentence is acting for itself or on itself. Because a reflexive pronoun must refer to a word in a sentence, it is not the subject or direct object. If used to show emphasis, reflexive pronouns are called *intensive pronouns.* (See section 14.)

Singular	Plural
First person: myself	First person: ourselves
Second person: yourself	Second person: yourselves
Third person: himself, herself, itself	Third person: themselves

She returned the book **herself** rather than giving it to her

(reflexive pronoun)

roommate to bring back.

Relative Pronouns Pronouns that show the relationship of a dependent clause to a noun in the sentence. Relative pronouns substitute for nouns already mentioned in sentences and introduce adjective or noun clauses.

Relative pronouns: that, which, who, whom, whose

This was the movie **that** won the Academy Award.

Restrictive Clauses and Phrases   See **Essential and Nonessential Clauses and Phrases.**

Run-on Sentences   See **fused sentences** and section 12.

Sentences   Groups of words that have at least one independent clause (a complete unit of thought with a subject and predicate). Sentences can be classified by their structure as simple, compound, complex, and compound-complex.

Simple: one independent clause
Compound: two or more independent clauses
Complex: one or more independent clauses and one or more dependent clauses
Compound-complex: two or more independent clauses and one or more dependent clauses

Sentences can also be classified by their function as declarative, interrogative, imperative, and exclamatory.

Declarative: makes a statement
Interrogative: asks a question
Imperative: issues a command
Exclamatory: makes an exclamation

Sentence Diagrams   A method of showing relationships within a sentence.

Marnie's **cousin,** who has no taste in food, **ordered** a **hamburger** with coleslaw at the Chinese restaurant.

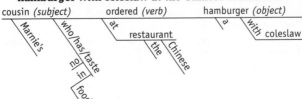

Sentence Fragment See **Fragment.**

Simple Sentence See **Sentence.**

Simple Tenses See **Verb Tenses.**

Split Infinitives Phrases in which modifiers are inserted between *to* and the verb. Some people object to split infinitives, but others consider them grammatically acceptable.

to quickly turn to easily reach   to forcefully enter

Subject   The word or words in a sentence that act or are acted upon by the verb or are linked by the verb to another word or words in the sentence. The *simple subject* includes only the noun or other main word or words, and the *complete subject* includes all the modifiers with the subject.

> **Harvey** objected to his roommate's alarm going off at 9 A.M. (*Harvey* is the subject.)

> **Every single one of the people in the room** heard her giggle. (The simple subject is *one;* the complete subject is the whole phrase.)

Subject Complement   The noun or adjective in the predicate (predicate noun or adjective) that refers to the same entity as the subject in sentences with linking verbs, such as *is/are, feel, look, smell, sound, taste,* and *seem.*

> She feels **happy.**   He is a **pharmacist.**
> ↗(subject complement)   ↗(subject complement)

Subject Case of Pronouns   See **Personal Pronouns** and section 14.

Subjunctive Mood   See **Mood.**

Subordinating Conjunctions   Words such as *although, if, until,* and *when,* that join two clauses and subordinate one to the other.

> She is late. She overslept.

> She is late **because** she overslept.

Subordination   The act of placing one clause in a subordinate or dependent relationship to another in a sentence because it is less important and is dependent for its meaning on the other clause.

Suffix   Word part added to the end of a word.

Suffix	Word
-ful	careful
-less	nameless

Superlative Forms of Adjectives and Adverbs   See **Adjectives** and **Adverbs** and section 15.

Synonyms   Words with similar meanings.

Word	Synonym
damp	moist
pretty	attractive

Tense   See **Verb Tense.**

Tone   The attitude or level of formality reflected in the word choices in a piece of writing. (See section 5.)

Transitions   Words in sentences that show relationships between sentences and paragraphs. (See section 9.)

Transitive Verbs   See **Verbs.**

Verbals   Words that are derived from verbs but do not act as verbs in sentences. Three types of verbals are infinitives, participles, and gerunds.

Infinitives   to + **verb**

  to wind   to say

Participles: Words used as modifiers or with helping
verbs. The present participle ends in *-ing,*
and many past participles end in *-ed.*

The dog is **panting.**   He bought only **used** clothing.
     (present participle)   (past participle)

Gerunds: Present participles used as nouns.

Smiling was not a natural act for her.
  (gerund)

Verbs Words or groups of words (verb phrases) in predicates that express action, show a state of being, or act as
a link between the subject and the rest of the predicate.
Verbs change form to show time (tense), mood, and voice
and are classified as transitive, intransitive, and linking
verbs. (See section 30.)

Transitive verbs: Require objects to complete the
predicate.

He **cut** the cardboard **box** with his knife.
  (transitive verb)   (object)

Intransitive verbs: Do not require objects.

My ancient cat often **lies** on the porch.
    (intransitive verb)

Linking verbs: Link the subject to the following noun or
adjective.

The trees **are** bare.
  (linking verb)

Verb Conjugations The forms of verbs in various tenses.
(See section 30.)

Regular:

Present

  Simple present:
I walk	we walk
you walk	you walk
he, she, it walks	they walk

  Present progressive:
I am walking	we are walking
you are walking	you are walking
he, she, it is walking	they are walking

  Present perfect:
I have walked	we have walked
you have walked	you have walked
he, she, it has walked	they have walked

  Present perfect progressive:
I have been walking	we have been walking
you have been walking	you have been walking
he, she, it has been walking	they have been walking

Past

Simple past:

I walked	we walked
you walked	you walked
he, she, it walked	they walked

Past progressive:

I was walking	we were walking
you were walking	you were walking
he, she, it was walking	they were walking

Past perfect:

I had walked	we had walked
you had walked	you had walked
he, she, it had walked	they had walked

Past perfect progressive:

I had been walking	we had been walking
you had been walking	you had been walking
he, she, it had been walking	they had been walking

Future

Simple future:

I shall walk	we shall walk
you will walk	you will walk
he, she, it will walk	they will walk

Future progressive:

I shall be walking	we shall be walking
you will be walking	you will be walking
he, she, it will be walking	they will be walking

Future perfect:

I shall have walked	we shall have walked
you will have walked	you will have walked
he, she, it will have walked	they will have walked

Future perfect progressive:

I shall have been walking	we shall have been walking
you will have been walking	you will have been walking
he, she, it will have been walking	they will have been walking

Irregular:

Present

Simple present:

I go	we go
you go	you go
he, she, it goes	they go

Present progressive:

I am going	we are going
you are going	you are going
he, she, it is going	they are going

Present perfect:

I have gone	we have gone
you have gone	you have gone
he, she, it has gone	they have gone

Present perfect progressive:

I have been going	we have been going
you have been going	you have been going
he, she, it has been going	they have been going

Past

    Simple past:

I went	we went
you went	you went
he, she, it went	they went

    Past progressive:

I was going	we were going
you were going	you were going
he, she, it was going	they were going

    Past perfect:

I had gone	we had gone
you had gone	you had gone
he, she, it had gone	they had gone

    Past perfect progressive:

I had been going	we had been going
you had been going	you had been going
he, she, it had been going	they had been going

Future

    Simple:

I shall go	we shall go
you will go	you will go
he, she, it will go	they will go

    Future progressive:

I shall be going	we shall be going
you will be going	you will be going
he, she, it will be going	they will be going

    Future perfect:

I shall have gone	we shall have gone
you will have gone	you will have gone
he, she, it will have gone	they will have gone

    Future perfect progressive:

I shall have been going	we shall have been going
you will have been going	you will have been going
he, she, it will have been going	they will have been going

Verb Phrases See **Verbs.**

Verb Tenses The times indicated by the verb forms in the past, present, or future. (For the verb forms, see **verb conjugations** and section 30.)

Present

    Simple present: Describes actions or situations that exist now and are habitually or generally true.

    I **walk** to class every afternoon.

    Present progressive: Indicates activity in progress, something not finished, or something continuing.

    He **is studying** Swedish.

    Present perfect: Describes single or repeated actions that began in the past and lead up to and include the present.

She **has lived** in Alaska for two years.

| **Present perfect progressive:** | Indicates action that began in the past, continues to the present, and may continue into the future. |

They **have been building** that garage for six months.

Past

| **Simple past:** | Describes completed actions or conditions in the past. |

They **ate** breakfast in the cafeteria.

| **Past progressive:** | Indicates past action that took place over a period of time. |

He **was swimming** when the storm began.

| **Past perfect:** | Indicates an action or event was completed before another event in the past. |

No one **had heard** about the crisis when the newscast began.

| **Past perfect progressive:** | Indicates an ongoing condition in the past that has ended. |

I **had been planning** my trip to Mexico when I heard about the earthquake.

Future

| **Simple future:** | Indicates actions or events in the future. |

The store **will open** at 9 A.M.

| **Future progressive:** | Indicates future action that will continue for some time. |

I **will be working** on that project next week.

| **Future perfect:** | Indicates action that will be completed by or before a specified time in the future. |

Next summer, they **will have been** here for twenty years.

| **Future perfect progressive:** | Indicates ongoing actions or conditions until a specific time in the future. |

By tomorrow, I **will have been waiting** for the delivery for one month.

Voice Verbs are either in the *active* or *passive* voice. In the active voice, the subject
performs the action of the verb. In the passive, the subject receives the action. (See section 7.)

The dog **bit** the boy.
        ↗ (active verb)

The boy **was bitten** by the dog.
        ↗ (passive verb)

Index

Correction Symbols

Symbol	Problem	Section
ab	abbreviation error	27
ad	adjective/adverb error	15
agr	agreement error	13
art	article	32
cap(s)	capitalization error	24
ca	case	14
cs	comma splice	12
dm	dangling modifier	16
frag	fragment	11
fs	fused/run-on sentence	12
hyph	hyphen	23
ital	italics	25
lc	lowercase	24
mix(ed)	mixed construction	6
mm	misplaced modifier	16
num	number use error	26
om	omitted word	34
//	parallelism error	8
p	punctuation error	18-23
pl	plural needed	31
ref	reference error	14
shft	shift error	17
sp	spelling error	28
t	verb-tense error	30
trans	transition needed	9
usage	usage error	Glossary of Usage
v	verb error	13, 30
var	variety needed	4
w	wordy	3
wc/ww	word choice/wrong word	5, 7, 10
x	obvious error	
^	insert	
∩ /tr	transpose	
℘	delete	

User's Guide